D0051442

¡Bienvenido!

Just Enough
SPANISH
HOW TO GET BY AND
BE EASILY UNDERSTOOD

New York Chicago San Francisco Lisbon London Madrid Mexico City
Milan New Delhi San Juan Seoul Singapore Sydney Toronto

The **McGraw·Hill** Companies

Library of Congress Cataloging-in-Publication Data

Ellis, D. L.
  Just enough Spanish / D. L. Ellis, R. Ellis ; pronunciation,
J. Baldwin.
    p.   cm.
  Includes index.
  ISBN 0-07-145141-2
  1. Spanish language—Conversation and phrase books—
English.   I. Ellis, R.   II. Title.

  PC4121.E62 2004
  468.3′421—dc22   2004061358

    8 9 10 11 12 13 14 15 16 17 18 19 20   DOC/DOC   0 9

ISBN 978-0-07-145141-3
MHID   0-07-145141-2

McGraw-Hill books are available at special quantity discounts to use
as premiums and sales promotions or for use in corporate training
programs. To contact a representative, please visit the Contact Us
pages at www.mhprofessional.com.

This book is printed on acid-free paper.

Contents

Using This Phrase Book

This phrase book is designed to help you get by in Spain—to get what you need or want. It concentrates on the simplest but most effective way that you can express your needs or desires in an unfamiliar language. While this phrase book may be generally useful in other Spanish-speaking countries, it is primarily intended for travelers to Spain.

The Contents tells you which section of the book to consult for the phrase you need. The Index has a more detailed list of topics that are covered in this book.

When you have found the correct page, you are given either the exact phrase you need or help in making a suitable sentence. You will also be given help in pronunciation. Especially helpful are the sections that provide the likely responses Spanish speakers may give to your questions.

To practice the basic nuts and bolts of the language further, we have included a "Do It Yourself" section at the end of the book.

The sections "Everyday Expressions," "Shop Talk," and "Public Notices" will be particularly useful, and you can expect to refer to them frequently.

Before you leave for Spain, be sure to contact one of the tourist information offices listed below (see page 15).

Spanish National Tourist Office
666 Fifth Avenue, 35th Floor
New York, NY 10103
(212) 265-8822 or (888) 657-7246

Mexican Government Tourist Office
405 Park Ave., Suite 1401
New York, NY 10022
(212) 755-7261

Venezuelan Consulate Office
7 East 51st Street
New York, NY 10022
(212) 826-1660

Argentine Consulate Office
12 W. 56th Street
New York, NY 10019
(212) 603-0400

A Note on Pronunciation

In the typical Spanish phrase book, there is a pronunciation key that tries to teach English-speaking tourists how to correctly pronounce Spanish. This is based on the belief that in order to be understood, the tourist must pronounce every word almost like a native speaker would.

The authors of this book set out to devise a more workable and more usable pronunciation system. We considered the fact that it is impossible for an average speaker of English, with no training in phonetics or phonetic transcription, to reproduce the sounds of a foreign language perfectly. Further, we believe that you don't have to have perfect pronunciation in order to make yourself understood in a foreign language. After all, native speakers will take into account that you are visitors to their country; they will most likely feel gratified by your efforts to communicate and will go out of their way to try to understand you. We have also found that visitors to a foreign country are not usually concerned with perfect pronunciation—they just want to get their message across, to communicate!

With this in mind, we have devised a pronunciation system of the utmost simplicity. This system does not attempt to give a tedious, problematic representation of Spanish sounds; instead, it uses common English sound and letter combinations that are closest to the sounds of Spanish. Since Spanish (like English) depends on one syllable in a word being stressed, we have put that stressed syllable in italics.

Practice makes perfect, so it is a good idea to repeat aloud to yourself the phrases you think you're going to use, before you actually use them. This will give you greater confidence and will help you to be understood.

You may want to pronounce Spanish as well as possible, of course, and the present system is an excellent way to start. Since it uses only the sounds of English, however, you will very soon need to depart from it as you imitate the sounds you hear Spanish speakers produce and begin to relate them to Spanish spelling. Fortunately, Spanish poses no problems in this regard, as there is an obvious and consistent relationship between pronunciation and spelling.

¡Diviértanse! Have fun!

Everyday Expressions

• See also "Shop Talk," p. 45.

Hello. **Hola.**
o·lah

Good morning. **Buenos días.**
bweh·nos dee·ahs

Good afternoon. **Buenas tardes.**
bweh·nahs tar·des

Good night. **Buenas noches.**
bweh·nahs no·ches

Good-bye. **Adiós.**
ah·dyos

See you later. **Hasta luego.**
ah·stah lweh·go

Yes. **Sí.**
see

Please. **Por favor.**
por fah·bor

Yes, please. **Sí, por favor.**
see por fah·bor

Great! **¡Estupendo!**
estoo·pen·do

Thank you. **Gracias.**
grah·thyahs

Thank you very much. **Muchas gracias.**
moo·chahs grah·thyahs

That's right. **Exacto.**
ex·ahc·to

No. **No.**
no

No, thank you. **No, gracias.**
no grah·thyahs

I disagree. **No estoy de acuerdo.**
no eh·stoy deh ah·cwehr·do

Excuse me./Sorry. **Perdone.**
pehr·do·neh

Don't mention it./That's okay. **De nada.**
deh nah·dah

That's good./I like it. **Está bien.**
eh·stah bee·en

That's no good./I don't like it. **No está bien.**
no eh·stah bee·en

2 Everyday Expressions

I know.	**Ya sé.** yah seh
I don't know.	**No sé.** no seh
It doesn't matter.	**No importa.** no im·*por*·tah
Where's the restroom, please?	**¿Dónde están los servicios,** **por favor?** don·deh eh·*stahn* los sehr·*bee*·thyos por fah·*bor*
How much is it?	**¿Cuánto es?** *cwahn*·to es
Is the tip included?	**¿Está incluido el servicio?** eh·*stah* incloo·ee·do el sehr·*bee*·thyo
Do you speak English?	**¿Habla usted inglés?** *ah*·blah oo·*sted* in·*glehs*
I'm sorry …	**Lo siento…** lo see·*en*·to
… I don't speak Spanish.	**no hablo español.** no *ah*·blo espah·*nyol*
… I only speak a little Spanish.	**sólo hablo un poco de español.** *so*·lo *ah*·blo oon *po*·co deh espah·*nyol*
… I don't understand.	**no comprendo.** no com·*pren*·do
Please, can you …	**Por favor, ¿puede…** por fah·*bor* pweh·deh
… repeat that?	**repetir eso?** rehpeh·*teer* eh·so
… speak more slowly?	**hablar más despacio?** ah·*blar* mahs des·*pah*·thyo
… write it down?	**escribirlo?** escri·*beer*·lo
What is this called in Spanish?	**¿Cómo se llama esto en español?** *co*·mo seh *yah*·mah *eh*·sto en espah·*nyol*

Crossing the Border

Essential Information

· Don't waste your time rehearsing what you're going to say to the border officials—chances are, you won't have to say anything at all, especially if you travel by air.

· It is more useful to check that you have the following documents ready for the trip: passport, airline tickets, money, traveler's checks, insurance documents, driver's license, and car registration documents.

· Look for the following signs.

Aduana	Customs
Frontera	Border
Funcionarios de Aduanas	Customs Officials
Control de Equipajes	Baggage Control

For additional signs and notices, see p. 115.

· You may be asked routine questions by the customs officials, such as those below. If you have to provide personal information, see "Meeting People," p. 5. It is important to know how to say "nothing": **Nada** (*nah*-dah).

Routine Questions

Passport?	**¿Pasaporte?** pahsah·*por*·teh
Insurance?	**¿Seguro?** seh·*goo*·ro
Registration papers?	**¿Cartilla de propiedad?** car·*tee*·yah deh pro·pyeh·*dahd*
Ticket, please.	**Billete, por favor.** bee·*yeh*·teh por fah·*bor*
Do you have anything to declare?	**¿Tiene algo que declarar?** tee·*en*·eh *ahl*·go keh declah·*rar*
Where are you going?	**¿Adónde va usted?** ah·*don*·deh bah oo·*sted*
How long are you staying?	**¿Cuánto tiempo va a quedarse?** *cwahn*·to tee·*em*·po bah ah keh·*dar*·seh
Where are you coming from?	**¿De dónde viene usted?** deh *don*·deh bee·*en*·eh oo·*sted*

You may also be required to fill out forms that ask for the following information.

apellido	last name
nombre	first name
nombre de soltera	maiden name
fecha de nacimiento	date of birth
lugar de nacimiento	place of birth
dirección	address
nacionalidad	nationality
profesión	profession
número de pasaporte	passport number
expedido en	issued at
firma	signature

Meeting People

See also "Everyday Expressions," p. 1.

Breaking the Ice

Hello.	**Hola.** *o*·lah
Good morning.	**Buenos días.** *bweh*·nos *dee*·ahs
How are you?	**¿Cómo está usted?** *co*·mo eh·*stah* oo·*sted*
Pleased to meet you.	**Mucho gusto.** *moo*·cho *goo*·sto
I am here …	**Estoy aquí…** eh·*stoy* ah·*kee*
… on vacation.	**de vacaciones.** deh bahcah·*thyo*·nes
… on business.	**de negocios.** deh neh·*go*·thyos
Can I offer you …	**¿Puedo ofrecerle…** *pweh*·do ofreh·*thehr*·leh
… a drink?	**una bebida?** *oo*·nah beh·*bee*·dah
… a cigarette?	**un cigarrillo?** oon thigah·*rree*·yo
… a cigar?	**un puro?** oon *poo*·ro
Are you staying long?	**¿Va a quedarse mucho tiempo?** bah ah keh·*dar*·seh *moo*·cho tee·*em*·po

Names

What's your name?	**¿Cómo se llama?** *co*·mo seh *yah*·mah
My name is _____.	**Me llamo _____.** meh *yah*·mo…

Family

Are you married?	**¿Es usted casado** (*male*)/ **casada** (*female*)**?** es oo·*sted* cah·*sah*·do/cah·*sah*·dah
I am …	**Soy…** soy
… married.	**casado** (*male*)/**casada** (*female*)**.** cah·*sah*·do/cah·*sah*·dah
… single.	**soltero** (*male*)/**soltera** (*female*)**.** sol·*teh*·ro/sol·*teh*·rah
This is …	**Le presento a…** le preh·*sen*·to ah
… my wife.	**mi esposa.** mee eh·*spo*·sah
… my husband.	**mi marido.** mee mah·*ree*·do
… my son.	**mi hijo.** mee *ee*·ho
… my daughter.	**mi hija.** mee *ee*·hah
… my (boy)friend.	**mi novio.** mee *no*·byo
… my (girl)friend.	**mi novia.** mee *no*·byah
… my (male/female) colleague.	**mi colega.** mee co·*leh*·gah
Do you have any children?	**¿Tiene hijos?** tee·*en*·eh *ee*·hos
I have …	**Tengo…** *ten*·go
… one daughter.	**una hija.** *oo*·nah *ee*·hah
… one son.	**un hijo.** oon *ee*·ho
… two daughters.	**dos hijas.** dos *ee*·hahs
… three sons.	**tres hijos.** tres *ee*·hos
No, I don't have children.	**No, no tengo hijos.** no no *ten*·go *ee*·hos

Where You Live

Are you …	**¿Es usted…**
	es oo·*sted*
… Spanish?	**español** (*male*)/**española** (*female*)?
	espah·*nyol*/espah·*nyo*·lah
… South American?	**sudamericano** (*male*)/
	sudamericana (*female*)?
	soodahmehri·*cah*·no/
	soodahmehri·*cah*·nah
I am …	**Soy…**
	soy
… American.	**americano** (*male*)/
	americana (*female*).
	ahmehri·*cah*·no/ahmehri·*cah*·nah

For other nationalities, see p. 129.

I live …	**Vivo…**
	bee·bo
… in New York.	**en Nueva York.**
	en *nweh*·vah york
… in the United States.	**en los Estados Unidos.**
	en los eh·*stah*·dos oo·*nee*·dos

For other countries, see p. 128.

… in the north.	**en el norte.**
	en el *nor*·teh
… in the south.	**en el sur.**
	en el soor
… in the east.	**en el este.**
	en el *eh*·steh
… in the west.	**en el oeste.**
	en el *weh*·steh
… in the center.	**en el centro.**
	en el *then*·tro

For the Businessman and Businesswoman

I'm from _____ (*company's name*).	**Soy de ____.** soy deh…
I have an appointment with _____.	**Tengo una cita con _____.** *ten*·go oo·nah *thee*·tah con…
May I speak to _____?	**¿Puedo hablar con _____?** *pweh*·do ah·*blar* con…

Here is my card.

Esta es mi tarjeta.
eh·stah es mee tar·*heh*·tah

I'm sorry I'm late.

Siento llegar tarde.
see·*en*·to yeh·*gar* tar·deh

Can I make another appointment?

¿Puedo fijar otra cita?
pweh·do fee·*har* o·trah *thee*·tah

I'm staying at the (Madrid) Hotel.

Estoy en el hotel (Madrid).
eh·*stoy* en el o·*tel* (mah·*dreed*)

I'm staying on (St. John's) Street.

Estoy en la calle (San Juan).
eh·*stoy* en la *cah*·yeh (sahn hwahn)

Asking Directions

Essential Information

- You will find the names of the following places on shops, maps, and public signs and notices.

What to Say

Excuse me, please.	**Perdone, por favor.**
	pehr·*do*·neh por fah·*bor*
How do I get …	**¿Para ir…**
	pah·rah eer
… to Madrid?	**a Madrid?**
	ah mah·*dreed*
… to Alfonso Primero Street?	**a la calle Alfonso Primero?**
	ah la *cah*·yeh ahl·*fon*·so pri·*meh*·ro
… to the Hotel Castilla?	**al Hotel Castilla?**
	ahl o·*tel* cah·*stee*·yah
… to the airport?	**al aeropuerto?**
	ahl ah·ehro·*pwehr*·to
… to the beach?	**a la playa?**
	ah la *plah*·yah
… to the bus station?	**a la estación de autobuses?**
	ah la estah·*thyon* deh
	ah·ooto·*boo*·ses
… to downtown?	**al centro?**
	ahl *then*·tro
… to the historic district?	**a la ciudad antigua?**
	ah la theeoo·*dahd* ahn·*tee*·gwah
… to the market?	**al mercado?**
	ahl mehr·*cah*·do
… to the police station?	**a la comisaría de policía?**
	ah la comisah·*ree*·ah deh
	poli·*thee*·ah
… to the port?	**al puerto?**
	ahl *pwehr*·to
… to the post office?	**a correos?**
	ah co·*rreh*·os
… to the train station?	**a la estación de tren?**
	ah la estah·*thyon* deh tren
… to the sports stadium?	**al estadio de deportes?**
	ahl eh·*stah*·dyo deh deh·*por*·tehs

How do I get …

¿Para ir…
pah·rah eer

… to the tourist information office?

a la oficina de información y turismo?
ah la ofi·*thee*·nah deh informah·*thyon* ee too·*rees*·mo

… to the town hall?

al ayuntamiento?
ahl ah·yoontahmee·*en*·to

Excuse me, please.

Perdone, por favor.
pehr·*do*·neh por fah·*bor*

Is there … nearby?

¿Hay… cerca?
ah·ee … *thehr*·cah

… an art gallery …

una galería de arte
oo·nah gahleh·*ree*·ah deh *ar*·teh

… a bakery …

una panadería
oo·nah pahnahdeh·*ree*·ah

… a bank …

un banco
oon *bahn*·co

… a bar …

un bar
oon bar

… a botanical garden …

un jardín botánico
oon har·*deen* bo·*tah*·nico

… a bus stop …

una parada de autobús
oo·nah pah·*rah*·dah deh ah·ooto·*boos*

… a butcher …

una carnicería
oo·nah carniteh·*ree*·ah

… a café …

una cafetería
oo·nah cafeteh·*ree*·ah

… a campsite …

un camping
oon *cahm*·ping

… a candy store …

una bombonería
oo·nah bomboneh·*ree*·ah

… a church …

una iglesia
oo·nah ee·*gleh*·syah

… a cinema …

un cine
oon *thee*·neh

… a currency exchange …

una oficina de cambio
oo·nah ofi·*thee*·nah deh *cahm*·byo

… a delicatessen …

una mantequería
oo·nah mahntekeh·*ree*·ah

… a dentist's office …

un dentista
oon den·*tee*·stah

Is there … nearby?	**¿Hay… cerca?**
	ah·ee … *thehr*·cah
… a department store …	**un almacén**
	oon ahlmah·*thehn*
… a disco …	**una discoteca**
	oo·nah disco·*teh*·cah
… a doctor's office …	**un consultorio médico**
	oon consool·*to*·rio *meh*·dico
… a drugstore …	**una farmacia**
	oo·nah far·*mah*·thyah
… a dry cleaner's …	**una tintorería**
	oo·nah tintoreh·*ree*·ah
… a fish market …	**una pescadería**
	oo·nah pescadeh·*ree*·ah
… a fruit market …	**una frutería**
	oo·nah frooteh·*ree*·ah
… a garage (*for repairs*) …	**un garaje**
	oon gah·*rah*·heh
… a gas station …	**una gasolinera**
	oo·nah gahsoli·*neh*·rah
… a grocery store …	**una tienda de comestibles**
	oo·nah tee·*en*·dah deh
	comeh·*stee*·bles
… a hairdresser's …	**una peluquería**
	oo·nah pelookeh·*ree*·ah
… a hardware store …	**una ferretería**
	oo·nah fehrrehteh·*ree*·ah
… a hospital …	**un hospital**
	oon ospi·*tahl*
… a hotel …	**un hotel**
	oon o·*tel*
… an ice-cream parlor …	**una heladería**
	oo·nah elahdeh·*ree*·ah
… a laundromat …	**una lavandería**
	oo·nah lahbahndeh·*ree*·ah
… a mailbox …	**un buzón**
	oon boo·*thon*
… a museum …	**un museo**
	oon moo·*seh*·o
… a newsstand …	**una tienda de periódicos**
	oo·nah tee·*en*·dah deh pehri·*o*·dicos
… a nightclub …	**una sala de fiestas**
	oo·nah *sah*·lah deh fee·*eh*·stahs

Is there … nearby?
¿Hay… cerca?
ah·ee … *thehr*·cah

… a park …
un parque
oon *par*·keh

… a parking lot …
un aparcamiento
oon aparcahmee·*en*·to

… a pastry shop …
una pastelería
oo·nah pahsteleh·*ree*·ah

… a pharmacy …
una farmacia
oo·nah far·*mah*·thyah

… a public garden (park) …
un jardín público
oon har·*deen* poo·blico

… a public restroom …
unos servicios públicos
oo·nos sehr·*bee*·thyos *poo*·blicos

… a restaurant …
un restaurante
oon restah·oo·*rahn*·teh

… a (snack) bar …
un bar
oon bar

… a Social Security Office …
una oficina de la Seguridad Social
oo·nah ofi·*thee*·nah deh la
segoori·*dahd* so·*thyahl*

… a sports field …
un campo de deportes
oon *cahm*·po deh deh·*por*·tehs

… a supermarket …
un supermercado
oon supehrmehr·*cah*·do

… a swimming pool …
una piscina
oo·nah pis·*thee*·nah

… a taxi stand …
una parada de taxis
oo·nah pah·*rah*·dah deh *tahx*·ees

… a telephone …
un teléfono
oon teh·*leh*·fono

… a theater …
un teatro
oon teh·*ah*·tro

… a tobacco shop …
un estanco
oon eh·*stahn*·co

… a travel agency …
una agencia de viajes
oo·nah ah·*hen*·thyah deh
bee·*ah*·hehs

… a youth hostel …
un albergue juvenil
oon ahl·*behr*·geh hooben·*eel*

… a zoo …
un zoo
oon *tho*·o

Directions

- Asking where a place is, or if a place is nearby, is one thing; making sense of the answer is another. Here are some of the most common directions and replies you will receive.

left	**izquierda** ith·*kyehr*·dah
right	**derecha** deh·*reh*·chah
straight ahead	**todo recto** *to*·do *rec*·to
there	**allí** ah·*yee*
first left/right	**la primera a la izquierda/derecha** la pri·*meh*·rah ah la ith·*kyehr*·dah/ deh·*reh*·chah
second left/right	**la segunda a la izquierda/derecha** la seh·*goon*·dah ah la ith·*kyehr*·dah/ deh·*reh*·chah
at the crossroad/intersection	**en el cruce** en el *croo*·theh
at the traffic light	**en el semáforo** en el seh·*mah*·foro
at the traffic circle	**en el cruce giratorio** en el *croo*·theh heerah·*to*·rio
at the grade crossing	**en el paso a nivel** en el *pah*·so ah ni·*bel*
It's near/far.	**Está cerca/lejos.** eh·*stah* thehr·cah/*leh*·hos
one kilometer	**a un kilómetro** ah oon ki·*lo*·metro
two kilometers	**a dos kilómetros** ah dos ki·*lo*·metros
Five minutes …	**A cinco minutos…** ah *theen*·co mi·*noo*·tos
… on foot.	**a pie.** ah pee·*eh*
… by car.	**en coche.** en *co*·cheh
Take …	**Tome…** *to*·meh
… the bus.	**el autobús.** el ah·ooto·*boos*

Take ...	**Tome...**
	to·meh
... the subway.	**el metro.**
	el *meh*·tro
... the train.	**el tren.**
	el tren

For public transportation, see p. 105.

The Tourist Information Office

Essential Information

- Most towns and many villages in Spanish-speaking countries have a tourist information office. Look for the following signs.

  Oficina de Información y Turismo
  Delegación Provincial de Información y Turismo
  Oficina Municipal de Información

- Sometimes there are signs with the following abbreviations.

  MIT (Ministerio de Información y Turismo)
  CITE (Centro de Iniciativas Turísticas Españolas)

- These offices provide free information in the form of leaflets, pamphlets, brochures, lists, transportation schedules, and maps. There may be a charge for some of these, but this is not typical.

- For finding a tourist information office, see p. 10.

What to Say

Please, do you have …	**Por favor, ¿tiene…** por fah·*bor* tee·*en*·eh
… a map of the town?	**un plano de la ciudad?** oon *plahn*·o deh la theeoo·*dahd*
… a list of bus tours?	**una lista de excursiones en autobús?** *oo*·nah *lee*·stah deh excoor·*syo*·nehs en ah·ooto·*boos*
… a list of campsites?	**una lista de campings?** *oo*·nah *lee*·stah deh *cahm*·pings
… a list of hotels?	**una lista de hoteles?** *oo*·nah *lee*·stah deh o·*teh*·les
… a list of restaurants?	**una lista de restaurantes?** *oo*·nah *lee*·stah deh restah·oo·*rahn*·tes
… a brochure on the town?	**un folleto de la ciudad?** oon fo·*yeh*·to deh la theeoo·*dahd*
… a brochure on the region?	**un folleto de la región?** oon fo·*yeh*·to deh la reh·hee·*on*
… a train schedule?	**un horario de trenes?** oon o·*rah*·rio deh *treh*·nes
… a bus schedule?	**un horario de autobuses?** oon o·*rah*·rio deh ah·ooto·*boo*·ses

In English, please.	**En inglés, por favor.** en in·*glehs* por fah·*bor*
How much do I owe you?	**¿Cuánto le debo?** *cwahn*·to leh *deh*·bo
Can you recommend …	**¿Puede recomendarme…** *pweh*·deh recomen·*dar*·meh
… an inexpensive hotel?	**un hotel barato?** oon o·*tel* bah·*rah*·to
… an inexpensive restaurant?	**un restaurante barato?** oon restah·oo·*rahn*·teh bah·*rah*·to
Can you make a reservation for me?	**¿Puede hacerme una reserva?** *pweh*·deh ah·*thehr*·meh *oo*·nah reh·*sehr*·bah

Likely Answers

- When the answer is "no," you should be able to tell by the person's facial expression, tone of voice, or gesture, but there are language clues, such as the following.

No.	**No.** no
I'm sorry.	**Lo siento.** lo see·*en*·to
I don't have a list of campsites.	**No tengo una lista de campings.** no *ten*·go *oo*·nah *lee*·stah deh *cahm*·pings
I don't have any more left.	**No me queda ninguno.** no meh *keh*·dah nin·*goo*·no
It's free.	**Es gratis.** es *grah*·tis

Accommodations

Hotel

Essential Information

- If you want hotel-type accommodations, look for the following signs.

  Hotel   Accommodation with all facilities, the quality depending on the star rating

  Hotel Residencia   Similar to a **hotel**, but often for longer stays

  Pensión   A small, privately run hotel

  Hostal/Fonda/Motel   A modest form of **pensión**

  Albergue   An often picturesque hotel in the countryside

  Parador   A converted palace or castle in a recognized beauty spot—relatively expensive

  The last two are run by the **Secretaría de Estado de Turismo** (Secretary of State for Tourism).

- In some places, you will find the following signs: **Camas** (beds), **Habitaciones** (rooms), **Casa** (house) followed by the owner's name, or **Casa de Huéspedes** (guest house). These are all alternatives to a **pensión**.

- Hotels are divided into five classes (from luxury to tourist class), and **pensiones** are divided into three.

- Lists of hotels and **pensiones** can usually be obtained from the local tourist information office (see p. 15).

- Since the price is displayed in the room itself, you can check it as you are looking at the room before agreeing to stay. The displayed price is for the room itself—per night, not per person. Breakfast is extra and therefore optional.

- Service and tax are always included in the price of the room, so tipping is optional. In Spain, however, it is normal practice to tip porters and waiters.

- Other than breakfast, not all hotels provide meals, apart from breakfast. A **pensión** always provides meals. Breakfast is continental style: coffee or tea, with rolls and jam.

- Some form of identification, like a passport or driver's license, is requested when you register at a hotel; the ID is normally kept overnight.

• To ask directions to a hotel, see p. 11.

What to Say

I have a reservation.	**Tengo una reserva.** *ten*·go *oo*·nah reh·*sehr*·bah
Do you have any vacancies, please?	**¿Tiene habitaciones libres, por favor?** tee·*en*·eh ahbeetah·*thyo*·nes *lee*·bres por fah·*bor*
Can I reserve a room?	**¿Puedo reservar una habitación?** *pweh*·do resehr·*bar* *oo*·nah ahbeetah·*thyon*
It's for …	**Es para…** es *pah*·rah
… one person.	**una persona.** *oo*·nah pehr·*so*·nah
… two people.	**dos personas.** dos pehr·*so*·nahs

For numbers, see p. 120.

It's for …	**Es para…** es *pah*·rah
… one night.	**una noche.** *oo*·nah *no*·cheh
… two nights.	**dos noches.** dos *no*·ches
… one week.	**una semana.** *oo*·nah seh·*mah*·nah
… two weeks.	**dos semanas.** dos seh·*mah*·nahs
I would like …	**Quiero…** kee·*eh*·ro
… a room …	**una habitación** *oo*·nah ahbeetah·*thyon*
… two rooms …	**dos habitaciones** dos ahbeetah·*thyo*·nes
… with a single bed.	**con una cama individual.** con *oo*·nah *cah*·mah indibi·*dwahl*
… with two single beds.	**con dos camas individuales.** con dos *cah*·mahs indibi·*dwah*·les
… with a double bed.	**con una cama doble.** con *oo*·nah *cah*·mah *do*·bleh
… with a toilet.	**con servicio.** con sehr·*bee*·thyo

I would like …	**Quiero…**
	kee·*eh*·ro
… a room …	**una habitación**
	oo·nah ahbeetah·*thyon*
… two rooms …	**dos habitaciones**
	dos ahbeetah·*thyo*·nes
… with a bathroom.	**con baño.**
	con *bahn*·yo
… with a shower.	**con ducha.**
	con *doo*·chah
… with a cot.	**con una cuna.**
	con *oo*·nah *coo*·nah
… with a balcony.	**con balcón.**
	con bahl·*con*
I would like …	**Quiero…**
	kee·*eh*·ro
… full board.	**pensión completa.**
	pen·*syon* com·*pleh*·tah
… half board.	**media pensión.**
	meh·dyah pen·*syon*
… bed and breakfast.	**desayuno incluido.**
	desah·*yoo*·no incloo·*ee*·do
Do you serve meals?	**¿Sirven comidas?**
	seer·ben co·*mee*·dahs
(At) what time is …	**¿A qué hora es…**
	ah keh *o*·rah es
… breakfast?	**el desayuno?**
	el desah·*yoo*·no
… lunch?	**la comida?**
	la co·*mee*·dah
… dinner?	**la cena?**
	la *theh*·nah
How much is it?	**¿Cuánto es?**
	cwahn·to es
Can I look at the room?	**¿Puedo ver la habitación?**
	pweh·do behr la ahbeetah·*thyon*
I would prefer a room …	**Prefiero una habitación…**
	preh·*fyeh*·ro *oo*·nah ahbeetah·*thyon*
… in the front/in the back.	**exterior/interior.**
	exteh·*ryor*/inteh·*ryor*
I would like a quiet room.	**Quiero una habitación tranquila.**
	kee·*eh*·ro *oo*·nah ahbeetah·*thyon*
	trahn·*kee*·lah

Okay, I'll take it.
Está bien, la tomo.
eh·*stah* bee·*en* la *to*·mo

No, thanks, I won't take it.
No, gracias, no la tomo.
no *grah*·thyahs no la *to*·mo

The key to number (10), please.
La llave de la número (diez), por favor.
la *yah*·beh deh la *noo*·mehro (dee·*eth*) por fah·*bor*

Please, may I have …
Por favor, ¿puede darme…
por fah·*bor* pweh·deh *dar*·meh

… an ashtray?
un cenicero?
oon thenee·*thehr*·o

… another blanket?
otra manta?
o·trah *mahn*·tah

… a coat hanger?
una percha?
oo·nah *pehr*·chah

… a glass?
un vaso?
oon *bah*·so

… another pillow?
otra almohada?
o·trah ahlmo·*ah*·dah

… some soap?
jabón?
hah·*bon*

… a towel?
una toalla?
oo·nah to·*ah*·yah

Come in!
¡Adelante!
adeh·*lahn*·teh

One moment, please!
¡Un momento, por favor!
oon mo·*men*·to por fah·*bor*

Please, can you …
Por favor, ¿puede…
por fah·*bor* pweh·deh

… do this laundry/dry cleaning?
lavar esto/limpiar esto en seco?
lah·*bar* eh·sto/lim·*pyar* eh·sto en *seh*·co

… call me at (seven o'clock)?
llamarme a (las siete)?
yah·*mar*·meh ah (las see·*eh*·teh)

… help me with my luggage?
ayudarme con el equipaje?
ah·yoo·*dar*·meh con el ehkee·*pah*·heh

… call me a taxi for (nine o'clock)?
llamarme un taxi para (las nueve)?
yah·*mar*·meh oon *tahx*·ee *pah*·rah (las *nweh*·beh)

For telling time, see p. 122.

The bill, please.	**La cuenta, por favor.** la *cwen*·tah por fah·*bor*
Is the tip included?	**¿Está incluido el servicio?** eh·*stah* incloo·*ee*·do el sehr·*bee*·thyo
I think this is wrong.	**Creo que esto está mal.** creh·o keh *eh*·sto eh·*stah* mahl
Can you give me a receipt?	**¿Puede darme un recibo?** *pweh*·deh *dar*·meh oon reh·*thee*·bo

AT BREAKFAST

Some more …, please.	**Más…, por favor.** mahs … por fah·*bor*
… coffee …	**café** cah·*feh*
… tea …	**té** teh
… bread …	**pan** pahn
… butter …	**mantequilla** mahnteh·*kee*·yah
… jam …	**mermelada** mehrmeh·*lah*·dah
May I have a boiled egg?	**¿Puedo haber un huevo pasado por agua?** *pweh*·do ah·*behr* oon *weh*·bo pah·*sah*·do por *ah*·gwah

Likely Reactions

Do you have any identification, please?	**¿Tiene usted un documento de identidad, por favor?** tee·*en*·eh oo·*sted* oon docoo·*men*·to deh identi·*dahd* por fah·*bor*
What's your name?	**¿Cómo se llama?** *co*·mo seh *yah*·mah
Sorry, we're full.	**Lo siento, está lleno.** Lo see·*en*·to eh·*stah* *yeh*·no
I don't have any rooms left.	**No me quedan habitaciones.** no meh *keh*·dahn ahbeetah·*thyo*·nes
Do you want to see the room?	**¿Quiere ver la habitación?** kee·*eh*·reh behr la ahbeetah·*thyon*
How many people is it for?	**¿Para cuántas personas es?** *pah*·rah *cwahn*·tahs pehr·*so*·nahs es

From (seven o'clock) onwards.	**Desde (las siete) en adelante.** *des*·deh (las see·*eh*·teh) en adeh·*lahn*·teh
From (midday) onwards.	**Desde (mediodía) en adelante.** *des*·deh (*meh*·dyo *dee*·ah) en adeh·*lahn*·teh

For telling time, see p. 122.

For telling time, see p. 122.

It's (30) euros.	**Son (treinta) euros.** son (*trayn*·tah) *eh*·ooros

For numbers, see p. 120.

Camping and Youth Hosteling

Essential Information

CAMPING

- Look for the word **Camping**.
- Be prepared to have to pay:

  per person
  for the car (if applicable)
  for the tent or trailer space
  for electricity
  for a hot shower

- You must provide proof of identity, such as your passport.

- In Spain, most campsites are located along the coast, and those inland are few and far between. You can camp off-site with the permission of the authorities and/or the landowner. However, there are a number of regulations that govern where you can or cannot camp—the Spanish Tourist Office in New York has details, so check with them before traveling abroad.

- Camping permits are no longer essential, but they are advisable because they provide third-party insurance for those camping off-site.

- During the peak season it is advisable to make reservations in advance by writing directly to the campsite.

- Persons under the age of sixteen are not admitted to a campsite unless accompanied by an adult.

YOUTH HOSTELS

- Look for the words **Albergue Juvenil**.

- You will be asked for your Youth Hostels Association (YHA) card and your passport upon arrival.

- Food and cooking facilities vary from hostel to hostel, and you may have to help with domestic chores.

- You must take your own sleeping bag lining, but bedding can sometimes be rented upon arrival.

- In peak season it is advisable to book beds in advance; your stay will be limited to a maximum of three consecutive nights per hostel.

- Apply to the Spanish Tourist Office in New York or to the local tourist offices in Spain (see p. 15) for lists of youth hostels and details of hostel regulations.

- For buying or replacing camping equipment, see p. 43.

What to Say

I have a reservation.	**Tengo una reserva.** *ten*·go *oo*·nah reh·*sehr*·bah
Do you have any vacancies?	**¿Tiene plazas libres?** tee·*en*·eh *plah*·thahs *lee*·bres
It's for …	**Es para…** es *pah*·rah
… one adult/one person …	**un adulto/una persona** oon ah·*dool*·to/*oo*·nah pehr·*so*·nah
… two adults/two people …	**dos adultos/dos personas** dos ah·*dool*·tos/dos pehr·*so*·nahs
… and one child.	**y un niño.** ee oon *nee*·nyo
… and two children.	**y dos niños.** ee dos *nee*·nyos
It's for …	**Es para…** es *pah*·rah
… one night.	**una noche.** *oo*·nah *no*·cheh
… two nights.	**dos noches.** dos *no*·ches
… one week.	**una semana.** *oo*·nah seh·*mah*·nah
… two weeks.	**dos semanas.** dos seh·*mah*·nahs

How much is it …
¿Cuánto es…
cwahn·to es

… for the tent?
por la tienda?
por la tee·*en*·dah

… for the camper?
por la caravana?
por la carah·*bahn*·ah

… for the car?
por el coche?
por el *co*·cheh

… for the electricity?
por la electricidad?
por la elec·*tree*·theedahd

… per person?
por persona?
por pehr·*so*·nah

… per day/night?
por día/noche?
por *dee*·ah/*no*·cheh

May I look around?
¿Puedo mirar?
pweh·do mee·*rar*

Do you close the gate/door at night?
¿Cierran la puerta por la noche?
thee·*ehr*·ahn la *pwehr*·tah por la *no*·cheh

Do you provide anything …
¿Dan ustedes algo…
dahn oo·*steh*·des *ahl*·go

… to eat?
de comer?
deh co·*mehr*

… to drink?
de beber?
deh beh·*behr*

Is there/Are there …
¿Hay…
ah·ee

… a bar?
bar?
bar

… hot showers?
duchas calientes?
doo·chahs cah·*lyen*·tes

… a kitchen?
cocina?
co·*thee*·nah

… a laundry room?
lavandería?
lahbahndeh·*ree*·ah

… a restaurant?
restaurante?
rehstah·oo·*rahn*·teh

… a shop?
tienda?
tee·*en*·dah

… a swimming pool?
piscina?
pis·*thee*·nah

… a carry-out restaurant?
tienda de comidas preparadas?
tee·*en*·dah deh co·*mee*·dahs prepah·*rah*·dahs

For food shopping, see p. 50.

For eating and drinking out, see p. 70.

I would like a pass for the shower.	**Quiero una ficha para la ducha.** kee·*eh*·ro oo·nah *fee*·chah *pah*·rah la *doo*·chah
Where are …	**¿Dónde están…** *don*·deh eh·*stahn*
… the garbage cans?	**los cubos de basura?** los *coo*·bos deh bah·*soo*·rah
… the showers?	**las duchas?** las *doo*·chahs
… the toilets?	**los servicios?** los sehr·*bee*·thyos
(At) what time must one …	**¿A qué hora debe uno…** ah keh *o*·rah *deh*·beh *oo*·no
… go to bed?	**acostarse?** ahco·*star*·seh
… get up?	**levantarse?** lehbahn·*tar*·seh
Please, do you have …	**Por favor, ¿tiene…** por fah·*bor* tee·*en*·eh
… a broom?	**una escoba?** *oo*·nah eh·*sco*·bah
… a can opener?	**un abrelatas?** oon ahbreh·*lah*·tahs
… a corkscrew?	**un sacacorchos?** oon sahcah·*cor*·chos
… any detergent?	**detergente?** dehtehr·*hen*·teh
… any dish detergent?	**lavavajillas?** lahbahbah·*hee*·yahs
… a dish towel?	**un paño de cocina?** oon *pah*·nyo deh co·*thee*·nah
… a fork?	**un tenedor?** oon teneh·*dor*
… a frying pan?	**una sartén?** *oo*·nah sar·*tehn*
… an iron?	**una plancha?** *oo*·nah *plahn*·chah
… a knife?	**un cuchillo?** oon coo·*chee*·yo
… a plate?	**un plato?** oon *plah*·to

Please, do you have …   **Por favor, ¿tiene…**
                                 por fah·*bor* tee·*en*·eh

… a refrigerator?   **un frigorífico?**
                                 oon frigo·*ree*·fico

… a saucepan?   **una cacerola?**
                                 oo·nah catheh·*ro*·lah

… a teaspoon?   **una cucharilla?**
                                 oo·nah coochah·*ree*·yah

The bill, please.   **La cuenta, por favor.**
                                 la *cwen*·tah por fah·*bor*

Problems

The faucet …   **El grifo…**
                                 el *gree*·fo

The razor outlet …   **El enchufe de la maquinilla de afeitar…**
                                 el en·*choo*·feh deh la mahki·*nee*·yah deh afay·*tar*

The toilet …   **El servicio…**
                                 el sehr·*bee*·thyo

… is not working.   **está roto.**
                                 eh·*stah ro*·to

The light …   **La luz…**
                                 la looth

The shower …   **La ducha…**
                                 la *doo*·chah

… is not working.   **está rota.**
                                 eh·*stah ro*·tah

My butane gas has run out.   **Mi camping gas se ha acabado.**
                                 Mee *cahm*·ping gahs seh ah ahcah·*bah*·do

Likely Reactions

Do you have any identification?   **¿Tiene usted un documento de identidad?**
                                 tee·*en*·eh oo·*sted* oon docoo·*men*·to deh identi·*dadd*

Your membership card, please.   **Su carné, por favor.**
                                 soo car·*neh* por fah·*bor*

What's your name?   **¿Cómo se llama?**
                                 co·mo seh *yah*·mah

Sorry, we're full.   **Lo siento, está lleno.**
                                 lo see·*en*·to eh·*stah yeh*·no

How many people is it for?	**¿Para cuántas personas es?**
	pah·rah cwahn·tahs pehr·so·nahs es
How many nights is it for?	**¿Para cuántas noches es?**
	pah·rah cwahn·tahs no·ches es
It's (10) euros …	**Son (diez) euros…**
	son (dee·eth) eh·ooros
… per day.	**por día.**
	por dee·ah
… per night.	**por noche.**
	por no·cheh

For numbers, see p. 120.

Rented Lodging

Essential Information

- If you're looking for lodging to rent, look for the following words in advertising and on signs.

Se alquila	For rent
Piso	Apartment with two or more bedrooms
Apartamento	One-bedroom apartment
Villa	Villa
Chalet	House
Casa de campo	Cottage
Finca	Country house

- For arranging the details of your rental, see "Hotel," p. 17.

- If you rent on the spot, you will need to know the following words.

deposit	**el depósito**
	el deh·po·sito
key	**la llave**
	la yah·beh

- Having arranged your accommodation and arrived with the key, check the basic amenities that you take for granted at home.

- *Electricity:* Voltage? You may need an adapter for razors and small appliances brought from home.

  Learn how to turn the lights on and off.

- *Gas:* Municipal (natural) gas or bottled gas? Butane gas must be kept indoors, and propane gas must be kept outdoors.

- *Stove:* Don't be surprised to find the grill inside the oven (or no grill at all); a lid covering the burners that lifts up to form a backsplash; or a combination of two gas burners and two electric burners.
- *Toilet:* Sewer drainage or septic tank? Don't flush disposable diapers or similar materials down the toilet if you have a septic tank.
- *Water:* Locate the shut-off valve. Check faucets and plugs—they may not operate the way you are used to. Be sure you know how to turn on (or light) the hot water heater.
- *Windows:* Learn how to open and close windows and shutters.
- *Insects:* Is an insecticide provided? If not, buy one.
- *Equipment:* See p. 43 for buying or replacing equipment.
- You will probably deal with a real estate agent, but find out whom to contact in an emergency; it may be a neighbor who is renting the lodging to you.

What to Say

My name is _____.	**Me llamo _____.** meh *yah*·mo…
I'm staying at _____.	**Estoy en _____.** eh·*stoy* en…
They have cut off …	**Han cortado…** ahn cor·*tah*·do
… the electricity.	**la electricidad.** la electrithee·*dahd*
… the gas.	**el gas.** el gahs
… the water.	**el agua.** el *ah*·gwah
Is there … in the area?	**¿Hay… en el área?** *ah*·ee … en el *ah*·reh·ah
… an electrician …	**un electricista** oon electri·*thee*·stah
… a plumber …	**un fontanero** oon fontah·*neh*·ro
… a gas man …	**un empleado de gas** oon empleh·*ah*·do del gahs
Where is …	**¿Dónde está…** *don*·deh eh·*stah*
… the furnace/boiler?	**la caldera?** la cahl·*deh*·rah

Where is …	**¿Dónde está…** *don·*deh eh·*stah*
… the fuse box?	**la caja de fusibles?** la *cah·*hah deh foo·*see·*bles
… the water heater?	**el calentador de agua?** el cahlentah·*dor* deh *ah·*gwah
… the water line shut-off valve?	**la llave de paso?** la *yah·*beh deh *pah·*so
Is there …	**¿Hay…** *ah·*ee
… municipal gas?	**gas ciudad?** gahs theeoo·*dahd*
… bottled gas?	**gas en botella?** gahs en bo·*teh·*yah
… a septic tank?	**cisterna?** thee·*stehr·*nah
… central heating?	**calefacción central?** cahlefahk·*thyon* then·*trahl*
The hair dryer …	**El secador…** el secah·*dor*
The immersion heater …	**El calentador de inmersión…** el cahlentah·*dor* deh inmehr·*syon*
The refrigerator …	**El frigorífico…** el frigo·*ree·*fico
The telephone …	**El teléfono…** el teh·*leh·*fono
The toilet …	**El servicio…** el sehr·*bee·*thyo
… is not working.	**está roto.** eh·*stah* ro·to
The stove (cooking) …	**La cocina…** la co·*thee·*nah
The heating system …	**La calefacción…** la cahlefahk·*thyon*
The iron …	**La plancha…** la *plahn·*chah
The pilot light …	**La luz del piloto…** la looth del pi·*lo·*to
The washing machine …	**La lavadora…** la lahbah·*do·*rah
… is not working.	**está rota.** eh·*stah* ro·tah

Where can I get …	**¿Dónde puedo obtener…**
	don·deh *pweh*·do obteh·*nehr*
… an adapter for this?	**un adaptador para esto?**
	oon ahdahptah·*dor pah*·rah *eh*·sto
… a fuse?	**un fusible?**
	oon foo·*see*·bleh
… insecticide?	**una insecticida en spray?**
	oo·nah insecti·*thee*·dah en *sprah*·ee
… a light bulb?	**una bombilla?**
	oo·nah bom·*bee*·yah
… a tank of butane gas?	**una botella de gas butano?**
	oo·nah bo·*teh*·yah deh gahs
	boo·*tah*·no
… a tank of propane gas?	**una botella de gas propano?**
	oo·nah bo·*teh*·yah deh gahs
	pro·*pah*·no
The drain …	**El desagüe…**
	el deh·*sah*·gweh
The toilet …	**El servicio…**
	el sehr·*bee*·thyo
… is stopped up.	**está atascado.**
	eh·*stah* ahtah·*scah*·do
The sink is stopped up.	**La fregadera está atascada.**
	la fregah·*dehr*·ah eh·*stah*
	ahtah·*scah*·dah
The gas is leaking.	**Hay un escape de gas.**
	ah·ee oon eh·*scah*·peh deh gahs
Can you repair it right away?	**¿Puede arreglarlo ahora mismo?**
	pweh·deh arreh·*glar*·lo ah·o·rah
	mees·mo
When can you repair it?	**¿Cuándo puede arreglarlo?**
	cwahn·do *pweh*·deh arreh·*glar*·lo
How much do I owe you?	**¿Cuánto le debo?**
	cwahn·to leh *deh*·bo
When is the garbage collected?	**¿Cuándo recogen la basura?**
	cwahn·do reh·*co*·hen la bah·*soo*·rah

Likely Reactions

What's your name?	**¿Cómo se llama?**
	co·mo seh *yah*·mah
What's your address?	**¿Cuál es su dirección?**
	cwahl es soo direc·*thyon*

There is a shop …
Hay una tienda…
 ah·ee *oo*·nah tee·*en*·dah

… in town.
en la ciudad.
 en la theeoo·*dahd*

… in the village.
en el pueblo.
 en el *pweh*·blo

I can't come …
No puedo ir…
 no *pweh*·do eer

… today.
hoy.
 oy

… this week.
esta semana.
 eh·stah seh·*mah*·nah

… until Monday.
hasta el lunes.
 ah·stah el *loo*·nes

I can come …
Puedo ir…
 pweh·do eer

… on Tuesday.
el martes.
 el *mar*·tes

… whenever you want.
cuando usted quiera.
 cwahn·do oo·*sted* kee·*eh*·rah

Every day.
Cada día.
 cah·dah *dee*·ah

Every other day.
Un día sin otro.
 oon *dee*·ah sin *o*·tro

On Wednesdays.
Los miércoles.
 los mee·*ehr*·coles

For days of the week, see p. 124.

General Shopping

The Drugstore

Essential Information

- Look for the word **Farmacia** or the signs at right.
- Prescription medicines are available only at a drugstore.
- Some nonprescription drugs can be bought at a supermarket or department store, as well as at a drugstore.

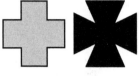

- Try the drugstore before going to the doctor; pharmacists are usually qualified to treat minor health problems.
- Normal business hours are 9 A.M.–2 P.M. and 5 P.M.–8 P.M.
- If the drugstore is closed, a notice on the door with the heading **Farmacias de Guardia** gives the address of the nearest drugstore that is open.
- Some toiletries can also be bought at a **perfumería**, but they will be more expensive there.
- For finding a drugstore, see p. 11.

What to Say

I would like …	**Quiero…** kee·*eh*·ro
… some Alka-Seltzer.	**Alka-Seltzer.** *ahl*·kah *selt*·thehr
… some antiseptic.	**antiséptico.** ahnti·*sep*·tico
… some aspirin.	**aspirinas.** ahspi·*ree*·nahs
… some bandages.	**vendas.** *ben*·dahs
… some Band-Aids.	**esparadrapo.** esparah·*drah*·po
… some cotton balls.	**algodón.** ahl·go·*don*
… some eyedrops.	**gotas para los ojos.** *go*·tahs *pah*·rah los *o*·hos

I would like …	**Quiero…**
	kee·*eh*·ro
… some foot powder.	**polvos para los pies.**
	pol·bos pah·rah los pee·*ehs*
… some sterile gauze.	**gasa.**
	gah·sah
… some inhalant.	**inhalante.**
	inah·*lahn*·teh
… some insect repellent.	**loción contra los insectos.**
	lo·*thyon* con·trah los in·*sec*·tos
… some lip balm.	**cacao para los labios.**
	cah·*cah*·o pah·rah los *lah*·byos
… some nose drops.	**gotas para la nariz.**
	go·tahs pah·rah la nah·*reeth*
… some throat lozenges.	**pastillas para la garganta.**
	pah·*stee*·yahs pah·rah la
	gar·*gahn*·tah
… some Vaseline.	**vaselina.**
	bahseh·*lee*·nah
I'd like something for …	**Quiero algo para…**
	kee·*eh*·ro *ahl*·go pah·rah
… bites/stings.	**las picaduras.**
	las picah·*doo*·rahs
… burns.	**las quemaduras.**
	las kehmah·*doo*·rahs
… a cold.	**el catarro.**
	el cah·*tah*·rro
… constipation.	**el estreñimiento.**
	el estrenyeemee·*en*·to
… a cough.	**la tos.**
	la tos
… diarrhea.	**la diarrea.**
	la deeah·*rreh*·ah
… an earache.	**el dolor de oído.**
	el do·*lor* deh o·*ee*·do
… flu.	**la gripe.**
	la *gree*·peh
… sore gums.	**el dolor de encías.**
	el do·*lor* deh en·*thee*·ahs
… hives.	**los sabañones.**
	los sahbah·*nyo*·nes
… sprains.	**las torceduras.**
	las thortheh·*doo*·rahs

I'd like something for … **Quiero algo para…**
kee·*eh*·ro *ahl*·go *pah*·rah

… sunburn. **las quemaduras de sol.**
las kehmah·*doo*·rahs deh sol

… travel sickness. **el mareo.**
el mah·*reh*·o

I need … **Necesito…**
netheh·*see*·to

… some baby food. **comida para niños.**
co·*mee*·dah *pah*·rah *nee*·nyos

… some contraceptives. **anticonceptivos.**
ahnticonthep·*tee*·bos

… some deodorant. **desodorante.**
desodo·*rahn*·teh

… some disposable diapers. **pañales de papel.**
pahn·*yahl*·es deh pah·*pel*

… some hand cream. **crema para las manos.**
creh·mah *pah*·rah las *mah*·nos

… some lipstick. **lápiz de labios.**
lah·peeth deh *lah*·byos

… some make-up remover. **crema limpiadora.**
creh·mah limpyah·*do*·rah

… some kleenex. **tisús.**
tee·*soos*

… some razor blades. **cuchillas.**
coo·*chee*·yahs

… some safety pins. **imperdibles.**
impehr·*dee*·bles

… some sanitary napkins. **compresas.**
com·*preh*·sahs

… some shaving cream. **crema de afeitar.**
creh·mah deh ah·fay·*tar*

… some soap. **jabón.**
hah·*bon*

… some suntan lotion/oil. **loción/aceite bronceador.**
lo·*thyon*/ah·*thay*·teh
bronteh·ah·*dor*

… some talcum powder. **polvos de talco.**
pol·bos deh *tahl*·co

… some tampons. **tampones.**
tahm·*po*·nes

… some (soft) toilet paper. **papel higiénico (suave).**
pah·*pel* ee·*hyeh*·nico (*swah*·beh)

I need …	**Necesito…**
	netheh·*see*·to
… some toothpaste.	**pasta de dientes.**
	pah·stah deh dee·*en*·tes

For other essential expressions, see "Shop Talk," p. 45.

Vacation Items

Essential Information

- Here are other places to shop at and signs to look for.

Librería-Papelería	Stationery
Fotografiá	Film
Material Fotográfico	Film

- The main department stores in Spain are the following.

| **Al Campo** | **El Corte Inglés** | **Hipercor** |
| **Carrefour** | **Eroski** | **Mercadona** |

What to Say

Where can I buy …?	**¿Dónde puedo comprar…?**
	don·deh pweh·do com·*prar*
I would like …	**Quiero…**
	kee·*eh*·ro
… a beach ball.	**una pelota para la playa.**
	oo·nah peh·*lo*·tah *pah*·rah la
	plah·yah
… a bucket.	**un cubo.**
	oon *coo*·bo
… an American newspaper.	**un periódico americano.**
	oon pehri·*o*·dico ahmehri·*cah*·no
… some envelopes.	**sobres.**
	so·bres
… a guidebook.	**una guía.**
	oo·nah *ghee*·ah
… a handbag/purse.	**un bolso.**
	oon *bol*·so
… a map (of the area).	**un plano (del área).**
	oon *plah*·no (del *ah*·reh·ah)
… a parasol.	**una sombrilla.**
	oo·nah som·*bree*·yah
… some postcards.	**postales.**
	po·*stah*·les

Where can I buy …? **¿Dónde puedo comprar…?**
*don·*deh *pweh·*do com·*prar*

I would like … **Quiero…**
kee·*eh·*ro

… a shovel. **una pala.**
*oo·*nah *pah·*lah

… a straw hat. **un sombrero de paja.**
oon som·*breh·*ro deh *pah·*hah

… a suitcase. **una maleta.**
*oo·*nah mah·*leh·*tah

… some sunglasses. **unas gafas de sol.**
*oo·*nahs *gah·*fahs deh sol

… an umbrella. **un paraguas.**
oon pah·*rah·*gwahs

… some writing paper. **papel de escribir.**
pah·*pel* deh escri·*beer*

I would like … [*show the camera*] **Quiero…**
kee·*eh·*ro

… a roll of color film … **un rollo en color**
oon *ro·*yo en co·*lor*

… a roll of black and white film … **un rollo en blanco y negro**
oon *ro·*yo en *blahn·*co ee *neh·*gro

… for prints. **para papel.**
pah·*rah pah·*pel

… for slides. **para diapositivas.**
pah·*rah deeaposi·*tee·*bahs

… for 12 (24/36) exposures. **de doce (veinticuatro/treinta y seis) fotos.**
deh *do·*theh (bayn·tee·*cwah·*tro/ trayn·*tah ee *seh·*is) *fo·*tos

… some batteries. **unas pilas.**
*oo·*nahs *pee·*lahs

This camera is broken. **Esta cámara está rota.**
*eh·*stah *cah·*mah·rah eh·*stah ro·*tah

The film is stuck. **El rollo está atascado.**
el *ro·*yo eh·*stah ahtah·*scah·*do

Please, can you …? **Por favor, ¿puede…**
por fah·*bor* *pweh·*deh

… develop/print this? **revelar/imprimir esto?**
rehbeh·*lar*/impri·*meer* eh·*sto*

… load the camera for me? **recargar mi cámara?**
rehcar·*gar* mee *cah·*mah·rah

For other essential expressions, see "Shop Talk," p. 45.

The Tobacco Shop

Essential Information

· Tobacco is sold where you see the sign at right, which is brown and yellow.

· A tobacco shop is called **Estanco** or **Tabacalera**.

· For asking if there is a tobacco shop nearby, see p. 12.

· All tobacco shops sell stamps, and you can mail your letters in some of them. They also sell lottery tickets and other items that are typically found in a stationery store.

· Cigarettes can also be purchased in bars and supermarkets or at newsstands and kiosks.

What to Say

A pack of cigarettes …	**Un paquete de cigarrillos…** oon pah·*keh*·teh deh thigah·*rree*·yos
… with filters.	**con filtro.** con *feel*·tro
… without filters.	**sin filtro.** seen *feel*·tro
… king-size.	**extra largos.** *ex*·trah *lar*·gos
… menthol.	**mentolados.** mento·*lah*·dos
Those up there …	**Esos de allí…** *eh*·sos deh ah·*yee*
… on the right.	**a la derecha.** ah la deh·*reh*·chah
… on the left.	**a la izquierda.** ah la ith·*kyehr*·dah
These. [*point*]	**Estos.** *eh*·stos
Cigarettes, please.	**Cigarrillos, por favor.** thigah·*rree*·yos por fah·*bor*
A carton.	**Un cartón.** oon car·*ton*
Two packs.	**Dos paquetes.** dos pah·*keh*·tes

Do you have ...	**¿Tiene...**
	tee·*en*·eh
... American cigarettes?	**cigarrillos americanos?**
	thigah·*rree*·yos ahmehri·*cah*·nos
... American pipe tobacco?	**tabaco de pipa americano?**
	tah·*bah*·co deh *pee*·pah
	ahmehri·*cah*·no
... rolling tobacco?	**picadura de tabaco?**
	picah·*doo*·rah deh tah·*bah*·co
... a package of pipe tobacco?	**un paquete de tabaco de pipa?**
	oon pah·*keh*·teh deh tah·*bah*·co
	deh *pee*·pah
That one down there ...	**Ese de allá abajo...**
	eh·seh deh ah·*yah* a·*bah*·ho
... on the right.	**a la derecha.**
	ah la deh·*reh*·chah
... on the left.	**a la izquierda.**
	ah la ith·*kyehr*·dah
This one. [*point*]	**Este.**
	eh·steh
That one. [*point*]	**Ese.**
	eh·seh
Those.	**Esos.**
	eh·sos
A cigar, please.	**Un puro, por favor.**
	oon *poo*·ro por fah·*bor*
Some cigars.	**Puros.**
	poo·ros
A box of matches.	**Una caja de cerillas.**
	oo·nah *cah*·hah deh theh·*ree*·yahs
A package of pipe-cleaners.	**Un paquete de escobillas.**
	oon pah·*keh*·teh deh esco·*bee*·yahs
A package of flints.	**Un paquete de piedras**
	de encendedor.
	oon pah·*keh*·teh deh pee·*eh*·drahs
	deh enthendeh·*dor*
Lighter fluid.	**Combustible para el encendedor.**
	comboo·*stee*·bleh *pah*·rah el
	enthendeh·*dor*

For other essential expressions, see "Shop Talk," p. 45.

Buying Clothes

Essential Information

- Look for the following signs.

Confecciones Señora	Women's Clothes
Lencería	Lingerie
Boutique Modas	Fashions
Confecciones Caballero	Men's Clothes
Sastrería-Panería	Men's Clothes
Zapatería/Calzados	Shoes

- Don't buy clothing without being measured first or trying the item on.
- Don't rely solely on conversion charts of clothing sizes (see p. 135).
- If you are buying clothing for someone else, take his or her measurements with you.
- Department stores (**almacenes** or **galerías**) all sell clothes and shoes.
- If you are interested in leather and fur articles look for a **Peletería** or **curtidos** or **artículos de piel**.

What to Say

I would like …	**Quiero…** kee·*eh*·ro
… a bathing suit.	**un traje de baño.** oon *trah*·heh deh *bahn*·yo
… a belt.	**un cinturón.** oon thintoo·*ron*
… a bikini.	**un bikini.** oon bi·*kee*·ni
… a blouse.	**una blusa.** oo·nah *bloo*·sah
… a bra.	**un sujetador.** oon soohehtah·*dor*
… a cap (swimming/ski).	**un gorro (de baño/de esquí).** oon *go*·rro (deh *bahn*·yo/ deh eh·*skee*)
… a cardigan.	**una chaqueta de punto.** *oo*·nah chah·*keh*·tah deh *poon*·to
… a coat.	**un abrigo.** oon ah·*bree*·go

I would like …
Quiero…
kee·*eh*·ro

… a dress.
un vestido.
oon beh·*stee*·do

… a hat.
un sombrero.
oon som·*breh*·ro

… a jacket.
una chaqueta.
oo·nah chah·*keh*·tah

… a nightgown.
un camisón.
oon cahmi·*son*

… a pair of pajamas.
un pijama.
oon pee·*hah*·mah

… a parka.
un anorak.
oon ahno·*rahk*

… a raincoat.
un impermeable.
oon impehrmeh·*ah*·bleh

… a shirt.
una camisa.
oo·nah cah·*mee*·sah

… a skirt.
una falda.
oo·nah *fahl*·dah

… a suit.
un traje.
oon *trah*·heh

… a sweater.
un jersey.
oon *hehr*·say

… a T-shirt.
una camiseta.
oo·nah cahmi·*seh*·tah

I would like a pair of …
Quiero un par de…
kee·*eh*·ro oon par deh

… briefs. [*women*]
bragas.
brah·gahs

… gloves.
guantes.
gwahn·tes

… jeans.
vaqueros.
bah·*keh*·ros

… shorts.
pantalones cortos.
pahntah·*lo*·nes *cor*·tos

… socks (short/long).
calcetines (cortos/largos).
cahltheh·*tee*·nes (*cor*·tos/*lar*·gos)

… stockings.
medias.
meh·dyahs

… tights.
leotardos.
leh·o·*tar*·dos

… trousers.
pantalones.
pahntah·*lo*·nes

I would like a pair of …	**Quiero un par de…**
	kee·*eh*·ro oon par deh
… underwear. [*men*]	**calzoncillos.**
	cahlthon·*thee*·yos
… shoes.	**zapatos.**
	thah·*pah*·tos
… canvas shoes.	**zapatos de lona.**
	thah·*pah*·tos deh *lo*·nah
… sandals.	**sandalias.**
	sahn·*dahl*·yahs
… beach sandals.	**playeras.**
	plah·*yeh*·rahs
… dress shoes.	**zapatos de vestir.**
	thah·*pah*·tos deh beh·*steer*
… boots.	**botas.**
	bo·tahs
… moccasins/loafers.	**mocasines.**
	mocah·*see*·nes
My (clothes) size is _____.	**Mi talla es _____.**
	mee *tah*·yah es…
My (shoe) size is _____.	**Mi número es _____.**
	mee *noo*·mehro es…
For numbers, see p. 120.	
For clothing sizes, see p. 135.	
Can you measure me, please?	**¿Puede medirme, por favor?**
	pweh·deh meh·*deer*·meh por
	fah·*bor*
Can I try it on?	**¿Puedo probármelo?**
	pweh·do pro·*bar*·mehlo
It's for a present.	**Es para un regalo.**
	es *pah*·rah oon reh·*gah*·lo
These are the measurements …	**Estas son las medidas…**
[*show written measurements*]	*eh*·stahs son las meh·*dee*·dahs
collar	**cuello**
	cweh·yo
bust	**busto**
	boo·sto
chest	**pecho**
	peh·cho
waist	**cintura**
	thin·*too*·rah

hip   **cadera**
cah·*deh*·rah

leg   **pierna**
pee·*ehr*·nah

Do you have something …   **¿Tiene algo…**
tee·*en*·eh *ahl*·go

… in black?   **en negro?**
en *neh*·gro

… in blue?   **en azul?**
en ah·*thool*

… in brown?   **en marrón?**
en mah·*rron*

… in green?   **en verde?**
en *behr*·deh

… in gray?   **en gris?**
en grees

… in pink?   **en rosa?**
en *ro*·sah

… in red?   **en rojo?**
en *ro*·ho

… in yellow?   **en amarillo?**
en ahmah·*ree*·yo

… in white?   **en blanco?**
en *blahn*·co

… in this color? [*point*]   **en este color?**
en *eh*·steh co·*lor*

… in cotton?   **en algodón?**
en ahlgo·*don*

… in denim?   **en dril?**
en dril

… in leather?   **en cuero?**
en *cweh*·ro

… in nylon?   **en nylon?**
en nee·*lon*

… in suede?   **en ante?**
en *ahn*·teh

… in wool?   **en lana?**
en *lahn*·ah

… in this material? [*point*]   **en este material?**
en *eh*·steh mahteh·*ryahl*

For other essential expressions, see "Shop Talk," p. 45.

Replacing Equipment

Essential Information

- Look for the following shops and signs.

Ferretería	Hardware
Electrodomésticos	Household appliances
Droguería	Store selling household goods and cleaning materials

- In a supermarket or department store look for the following signs.

  Hogar
  Artículos para el hogar
  Artículos de limpieza

- For asking directions to a shop, see p. 10.

- At a campsite, try its shop first.

What to Say

Do you have …	¿Tiene…
… an adapter? [*show appliance*]	**un adaptador?** oon ahdahptah·*dor*
… a bottle opener?	**un abrebotellas?** oon ahbrehbo·*teh*·yahs
… a can opener?	**un abrelatas?** oon ahbreh·*lah*·tahs
… a clothesline?	**un tendedero?** oon tendeh·*deh*·ro
… a corkscrew?	**un sacacorchos?** oon sahcah·*cor*·chos
… any detergent?	**detergente?** dehtehr·*hen*·teh
… any dish detergent?	**lavavajillas?** lahbahbah·*hee*·yahs
… a dish towel?	**un paño de cocina?** oon *pahn*·yo deh co·*thee*·nah
… any disinfectant?	**desinfectante?** desinfec·*tahn*·teh
… any disposable cups?	**vasos de plástico?** *bah*·sos deh *plah*·stico
… any disposable plates?	**platos de papel?** *plah*·tos deh pah·*pel*

Do you have …	**¿Tiene…**
… a flashlight?	**una linterna?**
	oo·nah lin·*tehr*·nah
… any flashlight batteries?	**pilas de linterna?**
	pee·lahs deh lin·*tehr*·nah
… any forks?	**tenedores?**
	teneh·*do*·res
… a fuse? [*show the one to be replaced*]	**un fusible?**
	oon foo·*see*·bleh
… insecticide?	**un insecticida en spray?**
	oon insecti·*thee*·dah en *sprah*·ee
… any knives?	**cuchillos?**
	coo·*chee*·yos
… a light bulb? [*show the one to be replaced*]	**una bombilla?**
	oo·nah bom·*bee*·yah
… a plastic bucket?	**un cubo de plástico?**
	oon *coo*·bo deh *plah*·stico
… a roll of paper towels?	**un rollo de papel de cocina?**
	oon *ro*·yo deh pah·*pel* deh co·*thee*·nah
… a scouring brush?	**un cepillo para fregar los platos?**
	oon theh·*pee*·yo *pah*·rah freh·*gar* los *plah*·tos
… a scouring pad?	**un estropajo?**
	oon estro·*pah*·ho
… a sponge?	**una esponja?**
	oo·nah es·*pon*·hah
… any string?	**cuerda?**
	cwehr·dah
… a tank of butane gas?	**una botella de gas butano?**
	oo·nah bo·*teh*·yah deh gahs boo·*tah*·no
… a tank of propane gas?	**una botella de gas propano?**
	oo·nah bo·*teh*·yah deh gahs pro·*pah*·no
… any tent pegs?	**estacas de camping?**
	eh·*stah*·cahs deh *cahm*·ping
… a universal plug (for the sink)?	**un tapón universal (para la fregadera)?**
	oon tah·*pon* oonibehr·*sahl* (*pah*·rah la fregah·*deh*·rah)
… a wrench?	**una llave inglesa?**
	oo·nah *yah*·beh in·*gleh*·sah

For other essential expressions, see "Shop Talk," p. 45.

Shop Talk

Essential Information

- Spain uses euro currency. Other Spanish-speaking countries use their own currency systems. Information is given below for Mexican currency as well as the Spanish euro system.

  Mexico (coins) 5, 10, 20, and 50 centavos; 1, 2, 5, 10, and 20 new pesos

  Mexico (bills) 10, 20, 50, 100, 200, and 500 new pesos

  Spain (coins) 1, 2, 5, 10, 20, and 50 céntimos; 1 and 2 euros

  Spain (bills) €5, €10, €20, €50, €100, €200, €500

CURRENCY CONVERTER

- Since the relative strengths of currencies vary, we cannot provide accurate exchange rates here. However, by filling in the charts below prior to your trip, you can create a handy currency converter.

PESOS	DOLLARS	EUROS		PESOS	DOLLARS	EUROS
_____	1	_____		5	_____	1
_____	2	_____		10	_____	2
_____	3	_____		25	_____	3
_____	4	_____		50	_____	4
_____	5	_____		100	_____	5
_____	10	_____		200	_____	10
_____	15	_____		300	_____	15
_____	25	_____		400	_____	20
_____	50	_____		500	_____	50
_____	75	_____		750	_____	100
_____	100	_____		1,000	_____	200
_____	250	_____		2,000	_____	500
				5,000	_____	1,000

- Important weights and measures follow.

50 grams	**cincuenta gramos** thin·*cwehn*·tah *grah*·mos
100 grams	**cien gramos** thee·*en grah*·mos
200 grams	**doscientos gramos** dos·thee·*en*·tos *grah*·mos
½ kilo	**medio kilo** *meh*·dyo *kee*·lo
1 kilo	**un kilo** oon *kee*·lo
2 kilos	**dos kilos** dos *kee*·los
½ liter	**medio litro** *meh*·dyo *lee*·tro
1 liter	**un litro** oon *lee*·tro
2 liters	**dos litros** dos *lee*·tros

For numbers, see p. 120.

- In small stores, don't be surprised if the customers, as well as the shop assistants, say "hello" and "good-bye" to you.

What to Say

CUSTOMER

Hello.	**Hola.** *o*·lah
Good morning.	**Buenos días.** *bweh*·nos *dee*·ahs
Good afternoon.	**Buenas tardes.** *bweh*·nas *tar*·des
Good-bye.	**Adiós.** ah·*dyos*
I'm just looking.	**Sólo estoy mirando.** *so*·lo eh·*stoy* mi·*rahn*·do
Excuse me.	**Perdone.** pehr·*do*·neh
How much is this/that?	**¿Cuánto es esto/eso?** *cwahn*·to es *eh*·sto/*eh*·so

What is that?	**¿Qué es eso?**
	keh es *eh*·so
What are those?	**¿Qué son esos?**
	keh son *eh*·sos
Is there a discount?	**¿Hay descuento?**
	ah·ee des·*cwehn*·to
I'd like that, please.	**Quiero eso, por favor.**
	kee·*eh*·ro *eh*·so por fah·*bor*
Not that.	**Eso no.**
	eh·so no
Like that.	**Así.**
	ah·*see*
That's enough, thank you.	**Basta, gracias.**
	bah·stah *grah*·thyahs
More, please.	**Más, por favor.**
	mahs por fah·*bor*
Less, please.	**Menos, por favor.**
	meh·nos por fah·*bor*
That's fine.	**Eso está bien.**
	eh·so eh·*stah* bee·*en*
Okay.	**Está bien.**
	eh·*stah* bee·*en*
I won't take it, thank you.	**No lo tomo, gracias.**
	no lo *to*·mo *grah*·thyahs
It's not right.	**No está bien.**
	no eh·*stah* bee·*en*
Thank you very much.	**Muchas gracias.**
	moo·chahs *grah*·thyahs
Do you have something …	**¿Tiene algo…**
	tee·*en*·eh *ahl*·go
… better?	**mejor?**
	meh·*hor*
… cheaper?	**más barato?**
	mahs bah·*rah*·to
… different?	**diferente?**
	deefehr·*en*·teh
… larger?	**más grande?**
	mahs *grahn*·deh
… smaller?	**más pequeño?**
	mahs peh·*keh*·nyo

(At) what time do you …	**¿A qué hora…** ah keh *o*·rah
… open?	**abren?** *ah*·bren
… close?	**cierran?** thee·*eh*·rrahn
Can I have a bag, please?	**¿Puedo tener una bolsa, por favor?** *pweh*·do ten·*ehr* oo·nah *bol*·sah por fah·*bor*
Can you give me a receipt?	**¿Puede darme un recibo?** *pweh*·deh *dar*·meh oon reh·*thee*·bo
Do you take …	**¿Toman ustedes…** to·mahn oo·*steh*·des
… American money?	**dinero americano?** di·*neh*·ro ahmehri·*cah*·no
… traveler's checks?	**cheques de viaje?** *cheh*·kes deh bee·*ah*·heh
… credit cards?	**tarjetas de crédito?** tar·*heh*·tahs deh *creh*·dito
I would like …	**Quiero…** kee·*eh*·ro
… one like that.	**uno así.** *oo*·no ah·*see*
… two like that.	**dos así.** dos ah·*see*

SHOP ASSISTANT

Can I help you?	**¿En qué puedo servirle?** en keh *pweh*·do sehr·*beer*·leh
What would you like?	**¿Qué desea/quiere?** keh deh·*seh*·ah/kee·*eh*·reh
Will that be all?	**¿Será eso todo?** seh·*rah* eh·so to·do
Is that all?	**¿Eso es todo?** *eh*·so es to·do
Anything else?	**¿Algo más?** *ahl*·go mahs
Would you like it wrapped?	**¿Quiere que se lo envuelva?** kee·*eh*·reh keh seh lo en·*bwel*·bah
I'm sorry, there are none left.	**Lo siento, no queda ninguno.** lo see·*en*·to no *keh*·dah neen·*goo*·no

I don't have any.	**No tengo.**
	no *ten*·go
I don't have any more.	**No tengo más.**
	no *ten*·go mahs
How many do you want?	**¿Cuántos quiere?**
	cwahn·tos kee·*eh*·reh
How much do you want?	**¿Cuánto quiere?**
	cwahn·to kee·*eh*·reh
Is that enough?	**¿Basta?**
	bah·stah

Shopping for Food

Bread

Essential Information

- For finding a bakery, see p. 10.
- Here are key words to look for.

Horno	Bakery
Panadería	Bakery
Panadero	Baker
Pan	Bread

- Nearly all supermarkets and general stores sell bread.
- **Panaderías**, as well as other stores, are open from 9 A.M. to 2 P.M. and from 5 P.M. to 8 P.M., closing at lunchtime. In popular resorts, stores often stay open all day.
- The most characteristic type of loaf is the **barra**, which is a wider version of the French baguette; it comes in different sizes according to weight.
- For any other type of loaf, just ask for **un pan** and point.
- You can buy milk in some bakeries; look for the sign **Lechería-Panadería.** Soft drinks, candy, and ice cream can also be bought here.
- It's quite normal in Spain to have your bread delivered; if you wish to take advantage of this service, just ask your local baker.

What to Say

Some bread, please.	**Pan, por favor.**
	pahn por fah·*bor*
A loaf (like that).	**Un pan (así).**
	oon pahn (ah·*see*)
One long loaf.	**Una barra.**
	oo·nah *bah*·rrah
Three loaves.	**Tres panes.**
	tres *pah*·nes
Four long loaves.	**Cuatro barras.**
	cwah·tro *bah*·rrahs

250 grams of …	**Doscientos cincuenta gramos de…**
	dos·thee·*en*·tos thin·*cwehn*·tah
	grah·mos deh
½ kilo of …	**Medio kilo de…**
	meh·dyo *kee*·lo deh
1 kilo of …	**Un kilo de…**
	oon *kee*·lo deh
A bag of …	**Un paquete de…**
	oon pah·*keh*·teh deh
… sliced bread.	**pan de molde.**
	pahn deh *mol*·deh
… toasted bread.	**pan tostado.**
	pahn to·*stah*·do
… brown bread.	**pan integral.**
	pahn inteh·*grahl*
A bread roll.	**Un panecillo.**
	oon pahneh·*thee*·yo
Four bread rolls.	**Cuatro panecillos.**
	cwah·tro pahneh·*thee*·yos
Four croissants.	**Cuatro croissants.**
	cwah·tro crwah·sahns
Can the bread be delivered?	**¿Puede traer el pan a casa?**
	pweh·deh trah·*ehr* el pahn a
	cah·sah

For other essential expressions, see "Shop Talk," p. 45.

Cakes

Essential Information

· Here are key words to look for.

Pastelería	Pastry Shop
Confitería	Confectionery (cakes and candy)
Pastelero	Cake and pastry maker
Pasteles	Cakes
Pastas	Pastries

· **Churrería**: a place to buy **churros**, a kind of fritter that can be eaten on its own as carry-out or dipped in hot thick chocolate. For the latter, you have to ask for **chocolate con churros**.

· **Cafetería**: a place where you can buy cakes and drinks. You can also have chocolate and **churros**. For ordering a drink, see p. 70.

· For finding a pastry shop, see p. 12.

What to Say

The type of cakes you find in the shops varies from region to region, but the most common ones are listed below.

a bun made of puff pastry covered with sugar icing and filled with cream	**una ensaimada** *oo*·nah ensah·ee·*mah*·dah
a candied egg yolk	**una yema** *oo*·nah *yeh*·mah
cupcakes (small sponge teacakes)	**magdalenas** mahgdah·*leh*·nahs
a finger-sized fritter	**un churro** oon *choo*·rro
a round fritter	**un buñuelo** oon boo·*nweh*·lo
marzipan	**el mazapán** el mahthah·*pahn*
a meringue	**un merengue** oon meh·*ren*·geh
nougat (can be hard or soft)	**turrón** too·*rron*
a ring-shaped roll (like a donut)	**una rosquilla** *oo*·nah ro·*skee*·yah
shortbread	**mantecado** mahnteh·*cah*·do

You usually ask for medium-sized cakes by the number you wish to buy.

One donut.	**Un donut.** oon *do*·noot
Two donuts, please.	**Dos donuts, por favor.** dos *do*·noots por fah·*bor*

Small cakes are bought by weight, and it is best to point to the selection you prefer.

200 grams of cream puffs.	**Doscientos gramos de pastelitos de crema.** dos·thee·*en*·tos *grah*·mos deh pahsteh·*lee*·tos deh *creh*·mah
400 grams of biscuits.	**Cuatrocientos gramos de galletas.** cwahtro·thee·*en*·tos *grah*·mos deh gah·*yeh*·tahs

You may want to buy a larger cake by the slice.

| One slice of apple cake. | **Un trozo de pastel de manzana.**
oon *tro*·tho deh pah·*stel* deh
mahn·*thah*·nah |

| Two slices of almond cake. | **Dos trozos de pastel de almendra.**
dos *tro*·thos deh pah·*stel* deh
ahl·*men*·drah |

Churros are bought by euros.

| Three euros of churros, please. | **Tres euros de churros, por favor.**
trays *eh*·ooros deh *choo*·rros
por fah·*bor* |

You may also want to ask for a variety of pastries.

| A selection, please. | **Pasteles variados, por favor.**
pah·*steh*·les bahree·*ah*·dos
por fah·*bor* |

For other essential information, see "Shop Talk," p. 45.

Ice Cream and Candy

Essential Information

- Here are key words to look for.

Helados	Ice cream
Heladero	Ice-cream maker/seller
Heladería	Ice-cream parlor
Horchatería	Ice-cream parlor that also sells soft drinks
Confitería	Candy and pastry shop
Bombonera	Candy shop
Confitero	Candy maker/seller
Pastelería	Pastry shop
Pastelero	Cake and pastry maker

- The best-known ice-cream brands in Spain are the following.

| **Cami** | **Italianos** |
| **Frigo** | **Mallorquina** |

- Pre-packaged candy is available in general stores and supermarkets as well as at kiosks and tobacco shops. It is also usually available in **panaderías** (bakeries), where you can buy ice cream as well.

What to Say

A … ice cream, please.	**Un helado de…, por favor.** oon eh·*lah*·do deh … por fah·*bor*
… chocolate …	**chocolate** choco·*lah*·teh
… coffee …	**café** cah·*feh*
… creamy …	**nata** *nah*·tah
… hazelnut …	**avellana** ahbeh·*yah*·nah
… lemon …	**limón** lee·*mon*
… mint …	**menta** *men*·tah
… nougat flavor …	**turrón** too·*rron*
… orange …	**naranja** nah·*rahn*·hah
… pistachio …	**mantecado** mahnteh·*cah*·do
… raspberry …	**frambuesa** frahm·*bweh*·sah
… strawberry …	**fresa** *freh*·sah
… tutti-frutti …	**tuttifrutti** tootee·*froo*·tee
… vanilla …	**vainilla** bah·ee·*nee*·yah
A single cone. [*specify flavor as above*]	**Uno sencillo.** *oo*·no sen·*thee*·yo
Two single cones.	**Dos sencillos.** dos sen·*thee*·yos
A double-dip cone.	**Uno doble.** *oo*·no *do*·bleh
A cone.	**Un barquillo.** oon bar·*kee*·yo
A popsicle.	**Un polo.** oon *po*·lo
A chocolate popsicle.	**Un polo de bombón.** oon *po*·lo deh bom·*bon*
A wafer.	**Un corte.** oon *cor*·teh

A lollipop.	**Un pirulí.**
	oon piroo·*lee*
A carton.	**Un tarro.**
	oon *tah*·rro
An ice cream cake.	**Una tarta helada.**
	oo·nah *tar*·tah eh·*lah*·dah
A package of ...	**Un paquete de...**
	oon pah·*keh*·teh deh
... chewing gum.	**chicle.**
	chee·cleh
100 grams of ...	**Cien gramos de...**
	thee·*en grah*·mos deh
200 grams of ...	**Doscientos gramos de...**
	dos·thee·*en*·tos *grah*·mos deh
... candy.	**caramelos.**
	cahrah·*meh*·los
... chocolates.	**bombones.**
	bom·*bo*·nes
... mints.	**caramelos de menta.**
	cahrah·*meh*·los deh *men*·tah
... toffees.	**pastillas de café con leche.**
	pah·*stee*·yahs deh cah·*feh* con *leh*·cheh

For other essential expressions, see "Shop Talk," p. 45.

In the Supermarket

Essential Information

- Here are key words to look for.

Supermercado	Supermarket
Autoservicio	Self-service grocery store
Alimentación general	General food store

- Outside the store, you may see the words **Spar** or **Vege**.
- Here are common signs at supermarkets.

Entrada	Entrance
Prohibida la entrada	No entry
Salida	Exit
Prohibida la salida	No exit
Sin salida	No exit
Salida sin compras	Exit without purchases

Caja	Check-out
En oferta	Special
Autoservicio	Self-service

- Supermarkets are open from 10 A.M. to 10 P.M. Small grocery stores are open from 9 A.M. to 2 P.M. and from 5 P.M. to 8 P.M.

- It is usually not necessary to say anything in a supermarket, but you should ask if you don't see what you want.

What to Say

Excuse me, please.	**Perdone, por favor.**
	pehr·*do*·neh por fah·*bor*
Where is …	**¿Dónde está…**
	don·deh eh·*stah*
… the bread?	**el pan?**
	el pahn
… the butter?	**la mantequilla?**
	la mahnteh·*kee*·yah
… the cheese?	**el queso?**
	el *keh*·so
… the chocolate?	**el chocolate?**
	el choco·*lah*·teh
… the coffee?	**el café?**
	el cah·*feh*
… the cooking oil?	**el aceite?**
	el ah·*thay*·teh
… the canned fish?	**el pescado en lata?**
	el peh·*scah*·do en *lah*·tah
… the fresh fish?	**el pescado?**
	el peh·*scah*·do
… the canned fruit?	**la fruta en lata?**
	la *froo*·tah en *lah*·tah
… the fruit?	**la fruta?**
	la *froo*·tah
… the jam?	**la mermelada?**
	la mehrmeh·*lah*·dah
… the meat?	**la carne?**
	la *car*·neh
… the milk?	**la leche?**
	la *leh*·cheh
… the mineral water?	**el agua mineral?**
	el *ah*·gwah meeneh·*rahl*

Where is …	**¿Dónde está…**
	*don·*deh eh·*stah*
… the salt?	**la sal?**
	la sahl
… the sugar?	**el azúcar?**
	el ah·*thoo·*car
… the tea?	**el té**
	el teh
… the vinegar?	**el vinagre?**
	el bee·*nah·*greh
… the wine?	**el vino?**
	el *bee·*no
… the yogurt?	**el yogurt?**
	el yo·*goor*
Where is/are …	**¿Dónde están…**
	*don·*deh eh·*stahn*
… the candy?	**los caramelos?**
	los cahrah·*meh·*los
… the cookies?	**las galletas?**
	las gah·*yeh·*tahs
… the eggs?	**los huevos?**
	los *weh·*bos
… the frozen foods?	**los congelados?**
	los conheh·*lah·*dos
… the fruit juices?	**los zumos de fruta?**
	los *thoo·*mos deh *froo·*tah
… the pastries?	**las pastas?**
	las *pah·*stahs
… the potato chips?	**las patatas fritas?**
	las pah·*tah·*tahs *free·*tahs
… the seafood?	**los mariscos?**
	los mah·*ree·*skos
… the soft drinks?	**las bebidas sin alcohol?**
	las beh·*bee·*dahs sin ahlco·*ol*
… the canned vegetables?	**las verduras en lata?**
	las behr·*doo·*rahs en *lah·*tah
… the vegetables?	**las verduras?**
	las behr·*doo·*rahs

For other essential expressions, see "Shop Talk," p. 45.

Picnic Food

Essential Information

- Here are key words to look for.

Charcutería	Delicatessen
Embutidos	Cold sausages
Fiambres	Cold meat, cold cuts
Tienda de Ultramarinos	Grocery store
Mantequería	Grocery store
Carnicería	Butcher

- In these shops, you can buy a wide variety of food, such as ham, salami, cheese, olives, appetizers, sausages, and freshly made carry-out dishes. Specialties vary from region to region.

- Here's a guide to the amount of prepared salad to buy.

  2–3 ounces/70 grams per person, if eaten as an appetizer to a substantial meal
  3–4 ounces/100 grams per person, if eaten as the main course of a picnic-style meal

What to Say

One slice of …	**Una rodaja de…**
	oo·nah ro·*dah*·hah deh
Two slices of …	**Dos rodajas de…**
	dos ro·*dah*·hahs deh
… ham.	**jamón de york.**
	hah·*mon* deh york
… cured ham, thinly sliced.	**jamón Serrano.**
	hah·*mon* seh·*rrah*·no
… pâté.	**paté.**
	pah·*teh*
… pork and beef cold meat.	**mortadela.**
	mortah·*deh*·la
… salami.	**salchichón.**
	sahlchee·*chon*
… spicy hard sausage.	**chorizo.**
	cho·*ree*·tho
… stuffed turkey.	**pavo trufado.**
	pah·bo troo·*fah*·do

100 grams of …	**Cien gramos de…** thee·*en grah*·mos deh
150 grams of …	**Ciento cincuenta gramos de…** thee·*en*·to thin·*cwehn*·tah *grah*·mos deh
200 grams of …	**Doscientos gramos de…** dos·thee·*en*·tos *grah*·mos deh
300 grams of …	**Trescientos gramos de…** tres·thee·*en*·tos *grah*·mos deh
… anchovies.	**anchoas.** ahn·*cho*·ahs
… cheese.	**queso.** *keh*·so
… olives.	**aceitunas.** ahthay·*too*·nahs
… Russian salad.	**ensalada rusa.** ensah·*lah*·dah *roo*·sah
… tomato salad.	**ensalada de tomate.** ensah·*lah*·dah deh to·*mah*·teh

You might also like to try some of the following foods.

pizza	**pizza** *peet*·sah
hot dog	**salchicha de Frankfurt** sahl·*chee*·chah deh Frahnk·*fort*
roast chicken	**pollo asado** *po*·yo ah·*sah*·do
blood sausage	**morcilla** mor·*thee*·yah
cheese sticks	**palitos de queso** pah·*lee*·tos deh *keh*·so
pork rinds	**cortezas** cor·*teh*·thahs
asparagus tips	**puntas de espárragos** *poon*·tahs deh eh·*spah*·rrahgos
smoked salmon	**salmón ahumado** sahl·*mon* ah·oo·*mah*·do
spiced sausage	**butifarra** booti·*fah*·rrah
highly seasoned sausage made with pork and herbs	**longaniza** longah·*nee*·thah
stuffed olives	**aceitunas rellenas** ahthay·*too*·nahs reh·*yeh*·nahs

black olives	**aceitunas negras**
	ahthay·*too*·nahs *neh*·grahs
potato chips	**patatas fritas**
	pah·*tah*·tahs *free*·tahs
gherkins	**pepinillos**
	pepi·*nee*·yos
crackers	**galletas saladas**
	gah·*yeh*·tahs sah·*lah*·dahs
sardines in oil	**sardinas en aceite**
	sar·*dee*·nahs en ah·*thay*·teh
tuna fish	**atún**
	ah·*toon*
farmer's cheese	**queso de Burgos**
	keh·so deh *boor*·gos
hard cheese from sheep's milk	**queso manchego**
	keh·so mahn·*cheh*·go
salted, smoked cheese made from sheep's milk	**queso de roncal**
	keh·so deh ron·*cahl*
a round-shaped, mild cheese	**queso de bola**
	keh·so deh *bo*·lah
goat cheese	**queso de cabra**
	keh·so deh *cah*·brah
a firm, mild cheese made from cow's milk	**queso de teta**
	keh·so deh *teh*·tah

For other essential expressions, see "Shop Talk," p. 45.

Fruits and Vegetables

Essential Information

- Here are key words to look for.

Verdura	Vegetables
Fruta	Fruit
Legumbres	Vegetables
Frutero	Fruit seller
Verdulería	Vegetable store
Frutería	Fruit store
Fresco	An indication of freshness

- If possible, buy fruit and vegetables at a market, where they are cheaper and fresher than in stores and shops. Open-air markets are held once or twice a week in most areas (sometimes daily in large towns), usually in the mornings.

- It is customary for you to choose your own fruit and vegetables at the market (and in some shops) and for the attendant to weigh and price them.
- Weight guide: One kilo of potatoes serves six people.

What to Say

250 grams of …	**Doscientos cincuenta gramos de…** dos·thee·*en*·tos thin·*cwehn*·tah *grah*·mos deh
½ kilo (about 1 pound) of …	**Medio kilo de…** *meh*·dyo *kee*·lo deh
1 kilo of …	**Un kilo de…** oon *kee*·lo deh
1½ kilos of …	**Un kilo y medio de…** oon *kee*·lo ee *meh*·dyo deh
2 kilos of …	**Dos kilos de…** dos *kee*·los deh
… apples.	**manzanas.** mahn·*thah*·nahs
… bananas.	**plátanos.** *plah*·tahnos
… cherries.	**cerezas.** theh·*reh*·thahs
… figs.	**higos.** *ee*·gos
… grapes (white/black).	**uvas (blancas/negras).** *oo*·bahs (*blahn*·cas/*neh*·grahs)
… oranges.	**naranjas.** nah·*rahn*·hahs
… pears.	**peras.** *peh*·rrahs
… peaches.	**melocotones.** mehloco·*to*·nes
… plums.	**ciruelas.** thee·*rweh*·lahs
… strawberries.	**fresas.** *freh*·sahs
… artichokes.	**alcachofas.** ahlcah·*cho*·fahs
… asparagus.	**espárrago.** eh·*spah*·rrahgo
… green beans.	**judías verdes.** hoo·*dee*·ahs *behr*·des

250 grams of …	**Doscientos cincuenta gramos de…**
	dos·thee·*en*·tos thin·*cwehn*·tah
	grah·mos deh
½ kilo (about 1 pound) of …	**Medio kilo de…**
	meh·dyo *kee*·lo deh
1 kilo of …	**Un kilo de…**
	oon *kee*·lo deh
1½ kilos of …	**Un kilo y medio de…**
	oon *kee*·lo ee *meh*·dyo deh
2 kilos of …	**Dos kilos de…**
	dos *kee*·los deh
… white lima beans.	**habas.**
	ah·bahs
… carrots.	**zanahorias.**
	thah·nah·*o*·ryahs
… leeks.	**puerros.**
	pweh·rros
… mushrooms.	**champiñones.**
	chahmpi·*nyo*·nes
… onions.	**cebollas.**
	theh·*bo*·yahs
… peas.	**guisantes.**
	ghee·*sahn*·tes
… potatoes.	**patatas.**
	pah·*tah*·tahs
… shallots.	**chalotes.**
	chah·*lo*·tes
… spinach.	**espinacas.**
	espi·*nah*·cahs
… tomatoes.	**tomates.**
	to·*mah*·tes
A pineapple, please.	**Una piña, por favor.**
	oo·nah *pee*·nyah por fah·*bor*
A grapefruit.	**Un pomelo.**
	oon po·*meh*·lo
A melon.	**Un melón.**
	oon meh·*lon*
A watermelon.	**Una sandía.**
	oo·nah sahn·*dee*·ah
A bunch of …	**Un puñado de…**
	oon poo·*nyah*·do deh
… parsley.	**perejil.**
	pereh·*heel*

A bunch of …	**Un puñado de…** oon poo·*nyah*·do deh
… radishes.	**rábanos.** *rah*·bahnos
A head of garlic.	**Una cabeza de ajo.** *oo*·nah cah·*beh*·thah deh *ah*·ho
A (head of) lettuce.	**Una lechuga.** *oo*·nah leh·*choo*·gah
A (head of) cauliflower.	**Un coliflor.** oon colee·*flor*
A (head of) cabbage.	**Un repollo.** oon reh·*po*·yo
A cucumber.	**Un pepino.** oon peh·*pee*·no
Like that, please.	**Así, por favor.** ah·*see* por fah·*bor*

The following fruits and vegetables may not be familiar to you.

chard (a kind of beet with edible stalks and leaves)	**acelgas** ah·*thel*·gahs
pumpkin (orange-colored fruit with edible layer next to rind)	**calabaza** cahlah·*bah*·thah
date plum (soft, sweet winter fruit like a large tomato)	**caqui** *cah*·kee
endive (a salad plant, also called "chicory")	**escarola** escah·*ro*·lah
pomegranate (a fruit, orange in color, with a lot of seeds)	**granada** grah·*nah*·dah
prickly pear (as its name suggests, the fruit of the cactus)	**higo chumbo** ee·go *choom*·bo
quince (a pear-shaped fruit used as a preserve)	**membrillo** mem·*bree*·yo
loquat (a small, slightly sour fruit, orange in color and juicy)	**níspero** *nee*·spehro

For other essential expressions, see "Shop Talk," p. 45.

Meat

Essential Information

- Here are key words to look for.

Carnicería	Butcher shop
Carnicero	Butcher

- Weight guide: 4–6 ounces/110–170 grams of meat serves one person.

- The figures on the opposite page can help you make sense of labels on counters and supermarket displays. Translations are often unhelpful, and you won't need to say the Spanish word.

What to Say

To buy a roast, first indicate the type of meat, then say how many people it is for.

Some beef, please.
Buey, por favor.
  bway por fah·*bor*

Some lamb/young lamb.
Cordero/ternasco.
  cor·*deh*·ro/tehr·*nah*·sco

Some mutton.
Carnero/oveja.
  Car·*neh*·ro/o·*beh*·hah

Some pork.
Cerdo.
  thehr·do

Some veal.
Ternera.
  tehr·*neh*·rah

A roast …
Un asado…
  oon ah·*sah*·do

… for two people.
para dos personas.
  pah·rah dos pehr·*so*·nahs

… for four people.
para cuatro personas.
  pah·rah *cwah*·tro pehr·*so*·nahs

… for six people.
para seis personas.
  pah·rah *seh*·is pehr·*so*·nahs

For steak, liver, kidneys, sausages, and ground meat, the same method of ordering applies.

Some steak, please.
Bistec, por favor.
  bi·*stehc* por fah·*bor*

Some liver.
Hígado.
  ee·gah·do

Beef **Buey**

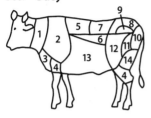

1 Cuello
2 Espaldilla
3 Pecho
4 Morcillo
5 Lomo alto
6 Solomillo
7 Lomo bajo
8 Tapa
9 Cadera
10 Redondo
11 Contra
12 Babilla
13 Falda con costillar
14 Chuleta

Veal **Ternera**

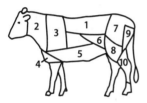

1 Lomo
2 Cuello
3 Espaldilla
4 Aleta o pecho
5 Falda
6 Riñonada
7 Cadera
8 Babilla
9 Contra
10 Morcillo (ossobuco)

Pork **Cerdo**

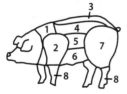

1 Aguja
2 Paletilla
3 Tocino
4 Chuletas o cinta
5 Magro para salchichas
6 Panceta
7 Jamón
8 Manos

Mutton **Carnero/oveja**

1 Lomo
2 Costillar
3 Falda
4 Pecina
5 Paletilla
6 Cuello
7 Manos

Some kidneys. **Riñones.**
ree·*nyo*·nes

Some sausages. **Salchichas.**
sahl·*chee*·chahs

Some ground meat … **Carne picada…**
car·neh pee·*cah*·dah

… for three people. **para tres personas.**
pah·rah tres pehr·*so*·nahs

… for five people. **para cinco personas.**
pah·rah *theen*·co pehr·*so*·nahs

For chops, order in the following way.

Two veal chops. **Dos escalopes de ternera.**
dos escah·*lo*·pes deh tehr·*neh*·rah

Three pork chops. **Tres chuletas de cerdo.**
tres choo·*leh*·tahs deh *thehr*·do

Four lamb chops. **Cuatro chuletas de cordero.**
cwah·tro choo·*leh*·tahs deh
cor·*deh*·ro

You may also want the following.

A chicken. **Un pollo.**
oon *po*·yo

A rabbit. **Un conejo.**
oon co·*neh*·ho

For other essential expressions, see "Shop Talk," p. 45.

Please, can you … **Por favor, ¿puede usted…**
por fah·*bor* *pweh*·deh oo·*sted*

… grind it? **picarlo?**
pee·*car*·lo

… dice it? **cortarlo en trozos?**
cor·*tar*·lo en *tro*·thos

… trim the fat? **quitar la grasa?**
kee·*tar* la *grah*·sah

Fish

Essential Information

- Look for the following sign.

  Pescadería   Fish market

- Another sign to look for is **Mariscos** (seafood).

- Markets and larger supermarkets usually have a fresh fish department.

- Weight guide: A minimum of 9 ounces/250 grams of fish on the bone serves one person. Use the following table as a guide.

¹/₂ kilo/500 grams	for 2 people
1 kilo	for 4 people
1¹/₂ kilos	for 6 people

What to Say

Purchase large fish and small shellfish by weight.

¹/₂ kilo of …	**Medio kilo de…**
	meh·dyo *kee*·lo deh
1 kilo of …	**Un kilo de…**
	oon *kee*·lo deh
1¹/₂ kilos of …	**Un kilo y medio de…**
	oon *kee*·lo ee *meh*·dyo deh
… clams.	**almejas.**
	ahl·*meh*·hahs
… cod.	**bacalao.**
	bahcah·*lah*·o
… hake.	**merluza.**
	mehr·*loo*·thah
… grouper.	**mero.**
	meh·ro
… mussels.	**mejillones.**
	mehee·*yo*·nes
… prawns.	**gambas.**
	gahm·bahs
… sardines.	**sardinas.**
	sar·*dee*·nahs
… shrimp.	**camarones/quisquillas.**
	cahmah·*ro*·nes/kee·*skee*·yahs
… turbot.	**rodaballo.**
	rodah·*bah*·yo

Some large fish can be purchased by the slice.

One slice of …	**Una rodaja de…**
	oo·nah ro·*dah*·hah deh
Two slices of …	**Dos rodajas de…**
	dos ro·*dah*·hahs deh
Six slices of …	**Seis rodajas de…**
	seh·is ro·*dah*·hahs deh
… cod.	**bacalao.**
	bahcah·*lah*·o
… salmon.	**salmón.**
	sahl·*mon*
… sea bream.	**besugo.**
	beh·*soo*·go
… fresh tuna.	**bonito.**
	bo·*nee*·to

For some shellfish and "frying pan" fish, specify the number you want.

One carp.	**Una carpa.**
	oo·nah *car*·pah
One crab, please.	**Un cangrejo, por favor.**
	oon cahn·*greh*·ho por fah·*bor*
One herring.	**Un arenque.**
	oon ah·*ren*·keh
One lobster.	**Una langosta.**
	oo·nah lahn·*go*·stah
One mackerel.	**Una caballa.**
	oo·nah cah·*bah*·yah
One octopus.	**Un pulpo.**
	oon *pool*·po
One plaice.	**Una platija.**
	oo·nah plah·*tee*·hah
One sole.	**Un lenguado.**
	oon len·*gwah*·do
One trout.	**Una trucha.**
	oo·nah *troo*·chah
One whiting.	**Una pescadilla.**
	oo·nah pescah·*dee*·yah

For other essential expressions, see "Shop Talk," p. 45.

Please can you …	**Por favor, ¿puede…**
	por fah·*bor* pweh·deh
… remove the heads?	**quitar las cabezas?**
	kee·*tar* las cah·*beh*·thahs

Please can you …

… clean them?

… filet them?

Por favor, ¿puede…
  por fah·*bor* pweh·deh
limpiarlos?
  lim·*pyar*·los
quitar la espina?
  kee·*tar* la eh·*spee*·nah

Eating and Drinking Out

Ordering a Drink

Essential Information

- Here are the places to ask for (see p. 10).

Cafetería	A more luxurious and modern café
Café	Generally an old-style, traditional café
Bar	A local establishment, suitable for families, that serves coffee, breakfast, soft drinks, and snacks, in addition to liquor

- If you want to try Spanish wine and **tapas** in a typically Spanish atmosphere, the places to go are: **una tasca, una bodega, un mesón,** or **una taberna.** Usually you'll find all these places in the same area, and it is the custom to make a tour of several local bars having one or two drinks in each.

- By law, the price list of drinks (**tarifa** or **lista de precios**) must be displayed outside or in the window.

- There is waiter service in all cafés, but you can drink at the bar or counter if you wish, which is cheaper.

- Always leave a tip of 10% to 15% of the bill unless you see **servicio incluido**; even so, it is still common practice to leave small change (a few euro cents) for a tip.

- Cafés serve both nonalcoholic drinks and alcoholic drinks, and they are usually open all day.

- You will find plates of assorted food, e.g., cheese, fish, olives, salads, etc., on the bar, usually before lunchtime or dinnertime. These are called **tapas**, and you can either have a portion (**una ración**) or food on sticks (**banderillas**). You have them as an aperitif or as a snack with your drink. As with drinks, you pay for **tapas** when leaving the bar, though some establishments offer small **tapas** free of charge.

What to Say

I'd like …, please.	**Quiero… por favor.** kee·*eh*·ro … por fah·*bor*
… black coffee …	**un café solo** oon cah·*feh* so·lo
… white coffee …	**un café con leche** oon cah·*feh* con *leh*·cheh
… black coffee with a dash of milk …	**un cortado** oon cor·*tah*·do
… tea …	**un té** oon teh
… with milk …	**con leche** con *leh*·cheh
… with lemon …	**con limón** con lee·*mon*
… a glass of milk …	**un vaso de leche** oon *bah*·so deh *leh*·cheh
… hot chocolate (thick) …	**un chocolate** oon choco·*lah*·teh
… mineral water …	**un agua mineral** oon *ah*·gwah meeneh·*rahl*
… lemonade …	**una limonada** *oo*·nah limo·*nah*·dah
… Coca-Cola …	**una Coca-Cola** *oo*·nah co·cah co·lah
… orangeade …	**una naranjada** *oo*·nah nahrahn·*hah*·dah
… orange juice …	**un zumo de naranja** oon *thoo*·mo deh nah·*rahn*·hah
… grape juice …	**un mosto** oon *mo*·sto
… pineapple juice …	**un zumo de piña** oon *thoo*·mo deh *peen*·yah
… a milkshake …	**un batido** oon bah·*tee*·do
… a beer …	**una cerveza** *oo*·nah thehr·*beh*·thah
… a draft beer …	**una caña** *oo*·nah *cahn*·yah
… cider …	**una sidra** *oo*·nah *see*·drah

A glass of …
Un vaso de…
oon *bah*·so deh

Two glasses of …
Dos vasos de…
dos *bah*·sos deh

… red wine.
vino tinto.
bee·no *teen*·to

… white wine.
vino blanco.
bee·no *blahn*·co

… rosé …
vino rosado
bee·no ro·*sah*·do

… dry.
seco.
seh·co

… sweet.
dulce.
dool·theh

… claret.
vino clarete.
bee·no clah·*reh*·teh

… sparkling wine.
vino espumoso.
bee·no espoo·*mo*·so

… champagne/cava.
champán/cava.
chahm·*pahn/cah*·bah

… sherry.
jerez.
heh·*rehth*

A whisky …
Un whisky…
oon *wee*·skee

… with ice.
con hielo.
con ee·*eh*·lo

… with water.
con agua.
con *ah*·gwah

… with soda.
con soda.
con *so*·dah

A gin …
Una ginebra…
oo·nah hee·*neh*·brah

… and tonic.
con tónica.
con *to*·nicah

… with lemon.
con limón.
con lee·*mon*

A brandy/cognac.
Un coñac.
oon *con*·yahc

A creme de menthe.
Una crema de menta.
oo·nah *creh*·mah deh *men*·tah

A coffee liqueur.
Una crema de café.
oo·nah *creh*·mah deh cah·*feh*

A rum.	**Un ron.**
	oon ron
A rum and coke.	**Un Cuba libre.**
	oon *coo*·bah *lee*·breh

Here are some local drinks you may like to try.

aniseed liqueur, served after meals or with cookies	**un anís**
	oon ah·*nees*
an iced drink, available in a variety of flavors	**un granizado**
	oon grahnee·*thah*·do
a drink made of nuts, water, and sugar	**una horchata**
	oo·nah or·*chah*·tah
a drink similar to sherry but lighter, an aperitif	**una manzanilla**
	oo·nah mahnthah·*nee*·yah
a sweet wine, served with dessert or cookies	**un moscatel**
	oon moscah·*tel*
red wine with bitter lemon, brandy, and sugar; can be drunk at any time, even with meals	**una sangría**
	oo·nah sahn·*gree*·ah
sweet wine, an aperitif	**vino de Málaga**
	bee·no deh *mah*·lahgah
spirit made from cocoa, taken after meals or with dessert	**crema de cacao**
	creh·mah deh cah·*cah*·o

Some other essential expressions are the following.

Miss! [*This does not sound abrupt in Spanish.*]	**¡Señorita!**
	senyo·*ree*·tah
Waiter!	**¡Camarero!**
	cahmah·*reh*·ro
The check, please.	**La cuenta, por favor.**
	la *cwehn*·tah por fah·*bor*
How much does that come to?	**¿Cuánto es?**
	cwahn·to es
Is the tip included?	**¿Está el servicio incluido?**
	eh·*stah* el sehr·*bee*·thyo incloo·*ee*·do
Where is the restroom, please?	**¿Dónde están los servicios, por favor?**
	don·deh eh·*stahn* los sehr·*bee*·thyos por fah·*bor*

Ordering a Snack

Essential Information

- Look for cafés or bars with the following signs.

Tapas	Appetizers
Bocadillos	Sandwiches
Meriendas	Afternoon snacks/meals

- You will find the names of snacks on signs in the window or on the sidewalk.

- In some regions, mobile vans sell hot snacks.

- For cakes, see p. 51.
  For ice cream, see p. 53.
  For picnic food, see p. 58.

What to Say

I would like …, please.	**Quiero…, por favor.**
	kee·*eh*·ro … por fah·*bor*
… a cheese sandwich …	**un bocadillo de queso**
	oon bocah·*dee*·yo deh *keh*·so
… a ham sandwich …	**un bocadillo de jamón de york**
	oon bocah·*dee*·yo deh hah·*mon* deh york
… a cured ham sandwich …	**un bocadillo de jamón serrano**
	oon bocah·*dee*·yo deh hah·*mon* seh·*rrah*·no

Here are some other snacks you may want to try.

spiced meatballs in tomato sauce	**albóndigas con tomate**
	ahl·*bon*·deegahs con to·*mah*·teh
savories on sticks	**banderillas**
	bahndeh·*ree*·yahs
cockles in brine	**berberechos**
	behrbeh·*reh*·chos
tripe, usually in hot paprika sauce	**callos**
	cah·yos
snails	**caracoles**
	cahrah·*co*·les
small pastries with a variety of fillings	**empanadillas**
	empahnah·*dee*·yahs
fried potatoes in spicy sauce	**patatas bravas**
	pah·*tah*·tas *brah*·bahs

stuffed peppers	**pimientos rellenos** pi·*myen*·tos reh·*yeh*·nos
Spanish omelet, made with potatoes and onions	**tortilla de patata** tor·*tee*·yah deh pah·*tah*·tah

For other essential expressions, see "Ordering a Drink," p. 70.

In a Restaurant

Essential Information

- The place to ask for is **un restaurante** (see p. 12).
- You can eat at any of the following places.

Restaurante	Restaurant
Cafetería	Luxurious café
Hostería/Mesón/ Parador/Posada	Regional cooking
Albergue de carretera	Roadside inn
Fonda	Cheap, simple food
Merendero	On the outskirts of town, suitable for meals or snacks during the early evening
Casa de comidas	A simple restaurant with typical Spanish home cooking

- You may also find **Casa** plus the name of the owner.
- Tipping is very common in Spain; it is typical to leave 10% of the bill for the waiter.
- By law, the menus must be displayed outside or in the window. That is the *only* way to judge if a place suits you before entering.
- Self-service restaurants (**autoservicio**) are not unknown, but all other places have waiter service.
- Restaurants are usually open from 1:00 P.M. to 3:00 or 3:30 P.M. and from 9:00 P.M. to 11:30 P.M., but this can vary. It's not difficult to get a meal before 9 P.M., because many restaurants, especially **casas de comidas** or **mesones,** provide meals in the early evening (**meriendas**). And if you want to eat before 1 P.M., you can always try some **tapas,** which can be a meal in themselves.
- By law, **hojas de reclamaciones** (complaint forms) must be posted in restaurants, as well as in hotels, bars, and gasoline stations. All complaints are investigated by the Tourist Authority.

What to Say

May I reserve a table?	**¿Puedo reservar una mesa?**
	pweh·do rehsehr·*bar oo*·nah *meh*·sah
I have reserved a table.	**He reservado una mesa.**
	eh rehsehr·*bah*·do *oo*·nah *meh*·sah
A table …	**Una mesa…**
	oo·nah *meh*·sah
… for one.	**para uno.**
	pah·rah *oo*·no
… for three.	**para tres.**
	pah·rah tres
The à la carte menu, please.	**El menú a la carta, por favor.**
	el meh·*noo* ah la *car*·tah por fah·*bor*
The fixed price menu.	**El menú de precio fijo.**
	el meh·*noo* deh *preh*·thyo *fee*·ho
The (8)-euro menu.	**El menú de (ocho) euros.**
	el meh·*noo* deh (o·cho) *eh*·ooros
The tourist menu.	**El menú turístico.**
	el meh·*noo* too·*ree*·stico
Today's special menu.	**El menú del día.**
	el meh·*noo* del *dee*·ah
The wine list.	**La lista de vinos.**
	la *lee*·stah deh *bee*·nos
What's this, please?	**¿Qué es eso, por favor?**
[*point to an item on the menu*]	keh es *eh*·so por fah·*bor*
A carafe of wine, please.	**Una jarra de vino, por favor.**
	oo·nah *hah*·rrah deh *bee*·no por fah·*bor*
A quarter (liter) (25 cc).	**Un cuarto.**
	oon *cwahr*·to
A half (liter) (50 cc).	**Un medio.**
	oon *meh*·dyo
A liter.	**Un litro.**
	oon *lee*·tro
A glass.	**Un vaso.**
	oon *bah*·so
A bottle.	**Una botella.**
	oo·nah bo·*teh*·yah
A half-bottle.	**Media botella.**
	meh·dyah bo·*teh*·yah

Red/white/rosé/house wine.

**Tinto/blanco/rosado/vino
de la casa.**
teen·to/*blahn*·co/ro·*sah*·do/*bee*·no
deh la *cah*·sah

Some more bread, please.

Más pan, por favor.
mahs pahn por fah·*bor*

Some more wine.

Más vino.
mahs *bee*·no

Some oil.

Aceite.
ah·*thay*·teh

Some vinegar.

Vinagre.
bee·*nah*·greh

Some salt.

Sal.
sahl

Some pepper.

Pimienta.
pi·*myen*·tah

Some water.

Agua.
ah·gwah

With/without garlic.

Sin/con ajo.
sin/con *ah*·ho

Miss! [*This does not sound
  abrupt in Spanish.*]

¡Señorita!
senyo·*ree*·tah

Waiter!

¡Camarero!
cahmah·*reh*·ro

The check, please.

La cuenta, por favor.
la *cwehn*·tah por fah·*bor*

How much does that come to?

¿Cuánto es?
cwahn·to es

Is the tip included?

¿Está incluido el servicio?
eh·*stah* incloo·*ee*·do el
sehr·*bee*·thyo

Where is the restroom, please?

¿Dónde está el servicio, por favor?
don·deh eh·*stah* el sehr·*bee*·thyo
por fah·*bor*

Here are some key words for meal courses, as seen on many menus.

What do you have in the way
  of …

¿Qué tiene de…
keh tee·*en*·eh deh

… appetizers?

entremeses?
entreh·*meh*·ses

… soup?

sopas?
so·pahs

… egg dishes?

huevos?
weh·bos

What do you have in the way of ...	¿Qué tiene de... keh tee-*en*-eh deh
... fish?	**pescados?** peh-*scah*-dos
... meat?	**carnes?** *car*-nes
... game?	**caza?** *cah*-thah
... fowl?	**aves?** *ah*-bes
... vegetables?	**verduras/legumbres?** behr-*doo*-rahs/leh-*goom*-bres
... cheese?	**queso?** *keh*-sos
... fruit?	**frutas?** *froo*-tahs
... ice cream?	**helados?** eh-*lah*-dos
... dessert?	**postres?** *po*-stres

Understanding the Menu

Essential Information

- The main ingredients of most dishes are given on the following pages.

Appetizers (p. 58)	Fruit (p. 60)
Meat (p. 64)	Cheese (p. 59)
Fish (p. 67)	Ice cream (p. 53)
Vegetables (p. 60)	Dessert (p. 51)

  Together with the following list of cooking and menu terms, the ingredient lists should help you decode a menu.

- These cooking and menu terms are for understanding only; for this reason, no pronunciation guide is given.

Cooking and Menu Terms

con aceite	in oil
en adobo	marinated in red wine
al ajillo	in garlic sauce
con ajolio (alioli)	in garlic mayonnaise
ahumado	smoked

en almíbar	in syrup
asado	roasted
a la barbacoa	barbecued
a la brasa	grilled over an open fire
en cacerola	casserole
caldo	stock
caliente	hot
cocido	boiled
crudo	raw
a la chilindrón	with tomatoes, peppers, and onion
dulce	sweet
en dulce	in sweet sauce
duro	hard-boiled
empanado	fried in breadcrumbs
en escabeche	marinated
escalfado	poached
estofado	braised/stewed
flameado	flambéed
a la francesa	with milk, flour, and butter
frío	cold
frito	fried
gratinado	browned with breadcrumbs or cheese
guisado	stewed
hervido	boiled
horneado	baked
al horno	baked
al jerez	in sherry
en su jugo	(roasted) in its juices
con mantequilla	with butter
marinado (a la marinera)	marinated
al minuto	prepared in a very short time
a la parrilla	grilled
pasado por agua	soft-boiled
con perejil	with parsley
a la pescadora	with egg, lemon, wine, and vinegar
a la plancha	grilled
rehogado	fried in oil with garlic and vinegar
relleno	stuffed
a la romana	deep fried
salado	salted
en salazón	cured

en salsa	in a sauce
en salsa blanca	in a white sauce
salsa mayonesa	in a mayonnaise sauce
salsa verde	sauce made from white wine, herbs, onion, and flour
salsa vinagreta	sauce made from salt, vinegar, and oil
salteado	sautéed
tostado	toasted
trufado	stuffed with truffles
al vapor	steamed
a la vasca	with asparagus, peas, egg, herbs, garlic, onion, and flour
en vinagre	in vinegar

Ingredients on Menus

anguilas	eels
arroz a la cubana	rice, fried eggs, bananas, and tomato sauce
arroz a la milanesa	rice with chorizo (spicy sausage), ham, cheese, and peas
atún	tuna fish
brazo de gitano	cake filled with cream or marmalade
buñuelos (buñuelitos)	small fritters with a variety of fillings
cabeza (de cordero)	(lamb's) head
caldereta	fish or lamb stew
callos (a la madrileña)	tripe in spicy sauce
cocido (madrileño)	vegetable and meat stew with beans or chickpeas
codorniz	quail
cochinillo asado	suckling pig, roasted
congrio	conger eel
conejo a la aragonesa	rabbit cooked with onion, garlic, almonds, and herbs
consomé	clear soup
criadillas	sweetbreads
cuajada	coagulated milk, similar to yogurt
pollo a la chilindrón	chicken fried with tomatoes, peppers, and smoked ham or bacon
potaje	vegetable stew
pote gallego	beans, meat, potatoes, and cabbage
puchero de gallina	stewed chicken

salmonete	red mullet
sesos	(lamb) brains
solomillo	tenderloin steak (of pork)
sopa Juliana	shredded vegetable soup
ternasco a la aragonesa	young lamb roasted with potatoes and garlic
tocino	bacon
toro de lidia	beef from the bullring
torrijas	French toast (bread dipped in milk and egg, then fried and sprinkled with sugar)
tortilla francesa	plain omelet
tortilla de patatas/española	traditional Spanish omelet made with potatoes
trucha a la navarra	trout filled with smoked ham
zarzuela	savory stew of assorted fish and shellfish

Health

Essential Information

- For details of reciprocal health agreements between your country and the country you are visiting, visit your local Department of Health office at least one month before leaving, or ask your travel agent.

- It is a good idea to purchase a medical insurance policy through a travel agent, an insurance broker, or a travel organization.

- Take an "emergency" first-aid kit with you.

- For minor health problems and treatment at a drugstore, see p. 32.

- For asking the way to a doctor, dentist, or drugstore, see pp. 10–11.

- In case of sudden illness or an accident, you can go to a **casa de socorro.** These are emergency first-aid centers open to the general public, and they are free. If you have a serious accident, the same free service is provided by an **equipo quirúrgico**. If you are on the road, there are **puestos de socorro** (first-aid centers) run by the **Cruz Roja** (Red Cross).

- It is sometimes difficult to get an ambulance. In an emergency you are legally entitled to drive over the speed limit, honking your horn and waving a white handkerchief, to the nearest hospital or first-aid center; other vehicles are required by law to give way to you. If you do not have a car, flag down a motorist.

- Once in the country, determine a plan of action in case of serious illness: Communicate your problem to a neighbor, the receptionist, or someone you see regularly. You are then dependent on that person to help you obtain treatment.

- To find a doctor in an emergency, look for **Médicos** in the Yellow Pages of the telephone directory. Here are important signs to look for.

Urgencia	Emergency room
Casa de Socorro/Puesto de Socorro	First-aid center
H/Hospital	Hospital

What Is the Matter?

I have a pain in my …

Me duele…
  meh *dweh*·leh

… abdomen.

el abdomen.
  el ahb·*do*·men

I have a pain in my …	**Me duele…** meh *dweh*·leh
… ankle.	**el tobillo.** el to·*bee*·yo
… arm.	**el brazo.** el *brah*·tho
… back.	**la espalda.** la eh·*spahl*·dah
… bladder.	**la vejiga.** la beh·*hee*·gah
… bowels.	**el vientre.** el bee·*en*·treh
… breast/chest.	**el pecho.** el *peh*·cho
… ear.	**el oído.** el o·*ee*·do
… eye.	**el ojo.** el *o*·ho
… foot.	**el pie.** el pee·*eh*
… head.	**la cabeza.** la cah·*beh*·thah
… heel.	**el talón.** el tah·*lon*
… jaw.	**la mandíbula.** la mahn·*dee*·boolah
… kidney.	**el riñón.** el ree·*nyon*
… leg.	**la pierna.** la pee·*ehr*·nah
… lung.	**el pulmón.** el pool·*mon*
… neck.	**el cuello.** el *cweh*·yo
… penis.	**el pene.** el *peh*·neh
… shoulder.	**el hombro.** el *om*·bro
… stomach.	**el estómago.** el eh·*sto*·mahgo
… testicle.	**el testículo.** el teh·*stee*·coolo
… throat.	**la garganta.** la gar·*gahn*·tah

I have a pain in my …	**Me duele…** meh *dweh*·leh
… vagina.	**la vagina.** la bah·*hee*·nah
… wrist.	**la muñeca.** la moo·*nyeh*·kah
I have a pain here. [*point*]	**Me duele aquí.** meh *dweh*·leh ah·*kee*
I have a toothache.	**Me duelen las muelas.** meh *dweh*·len las *mweh*·lahs
I have broken …	**Me he roto…** meh eh *ro*·to
… my dentures.	**la dentadura.** la dentah·*doo*·rah
… my glasses.	**las gafas.** las *gah*·fahs
I have lost …	**He perdido…** eh pehr·*dee*·do
… my contact lenses.	**mis lentes de contacto.** mis *len*·tes deh con·*tahc*·to
… a filling.	**un empaste.** oon em·*pah*·steh
My son is ill.	**Mi hijo está enfermo.** mee *ee*·ho eh·*stah* en·*fehr*·mo
My daughter is ill.	**Mi hija está enferma.** mee *ee*·hah eh·*stah* en·*fehr*·mah
He/she has a pain in his/her …	**Le duele…** leh *dweh*·leh
… ankle. [*see list above*]	**el tobillo.** el to·*bee*·yo

How Bad Is It?

I am ill.	**Estoy enfermo** (*male*)/ **enferma** (*female*). eh·*stoy* en·*fehr*·mo/en·*fehr*·mah
It is urgent.	**Es urgente.** es oor·*hen*·teh
It is serious.	**Es grave.** es *grah*·beh
It is not serious.	**No es grave.** no es *grah*·beh

It hurts.
Me duele.
meh *dweh*·leh

It hurts a lot.
Me duele mucho.
meh *dweh*·leh *moo*·cho

It does not hurt much.
No me duele mucho.
no meh *dweh*·leh *moo*·cho

The pain occurs …
El dolor ocurre…
el do·*lor* o·*coo*·reh

… every quarter of an hour.
cada cuarto de hora.
cah·dah *cwahr*·to deh o·rah

… every half hour.
cada media hora.
cah·dah *meh*·dyah o·rah

… every hour.
cada hora.
cah·dah o·rah

… every day.
cada día.
cah·dah *dee*·ah

It hurts most of the time.
Me duele casi todo el tiempo.
meh *dweh*·leh *cah*·see *to*·do el
tee·*em*·po

I have had it for …
Lo tengo desde hace…
lo *ten*·go *des*·deh *ah*·theh

… one hour/one day.
una hora/un día.
oo·nah o·rah/oon *dee*·ah

… two hours/two days.
dos horas/dos días.
dos o·rahs/dos *dee*·ahs

It is a …
Es un…
es oon

… sharp pain.
dolor agudo.
do·*lor* ah·*goo*·do

… dull ache.
dolor sordo.
do·*lor* *sor*·do

… nagging pain.
dolor continuo.
do·*lor* con·*tee*·nwo

I feel …
Me siento…
meh see·*en*·to

… dizzy.
mareado.
mahreh·*ah*·do

… feverish.
con fiebre.
con fee·*eh*·breh

… sick.
mareado (con nauseas).
mahreh·*ah*·do (con *nah*·oosyahs)

… weak.
débil.
deh·beel

Are you already being treated for something else?

I take … regularly.	**Tomo… regularmente.**
[show medication]	to·mo … rehgoolar·men·teh
… this medicine …	**esta medicina**
	eh·stah mehdi·thee·nah
… these pills …	**estas píldoras**
	eh·stahs peel·dorahs
I have …	**Tengo…**
	ten·go
… hemorrhoids.	**hemorroides.**
	eh·mo·roy·des
… rheumatism.	**reuma.**
	reh·oomah
I have a heart condition.	**Estoy del corazón.**
	eh·stoy del corah·thon
I am …	**Soy…**
	soy
… allergic to (penicillin).	**alérgico** (male)/**alérgica** (female)
	a (la penicilina).
	soy ah·lehr·heeco/ah·lehr·heecah
	ah (la penithi·lee·nah)
… asthmatic.	**asmático** (male)/**asmática** (female).
	ahs·mah·tico/ahs·mah·ticah
… diabetic.	**diabético** (male)/**diabética** (female).
	deeah·beh·tico/deeah·beh·ticah
I am pregnant.	**Estoy embarazada.**
	eh·stoy embarah·thah·dah

Other Essential Expressions

Please, can you help?	**Por favor, ¿puede ayudar?**
	por fah·bor pweh·deh ah·yoo·dar
A doctor, please.	**Un doctor, por favor.**
	oon doc·tor por fah·bor
A dentist.	**Un dentista.**
	oon den·tee·stah
I don't speak Spanish.	**No hablo español.**
	no ah·blo espah·nyol
(At) what time does … arrive?	**¿A qué hora llega…**
	ah keh o·rah yeh·gah
… the doctor …	**el doctor?**
	el doc·tor
… the dentist …	**el dentista?**
	el den·tee·stah

Here are important things the doctor may tell you.

Take this …	**Tome esto…** *to*·meh *eh*·sto
… every day.	**cada día.** *cah*·dah *dee*·ah
… every hour.	**cada hora.** *cah*·dah *o*·rah
… twice/four times a day.	**dos/cuatro veces al día.** dos/*cwah*·tro *beh*·thes ahl *dee*·ah
Stay in bed.	**Guarde cama.** *gwar*·deh *cah*·mah
Don't travel for _____ days/weeks.	**No viaje hasta dentro de** _____ **días/semanas.** no bee·*ah*·heh *ah*·stah *den*·tro deh … *dee*·ahs/seh·*mah*·nahs
You must go to the hospital.	**Tiene que ir al hospital.** tee·*en*·eh keh eer ahl ospi·*tahl*

Problems: Complaints, Loss, and Theft

Essential Information

- If you have problems with ...
    ... camping facilities, see p. 22.
    ... household appliances, see p. 43.
    ... your health, see p. 82.
    ... a car, see p. 98.

- If worse comes to worst, find the police station. To ask directions, see p. 9.

- Look for the following signs.

Comisaría de Policía	Police station
Cuartel de la Guardia Civil	Civil Guard (in small towns and villages)
Oficina de objetos perdidos	Lost and found

- If you lose your passport, go to your nearest Consulate.

- In an emergency, dial 091 for the police. The numbers for fire and ambulance differ by region. Remember, however, that the ambulance service is not free, nor are emergency calls from public phones.

Complaints

I bought this ...	**Compré esto...** com·*preh* eh·sto
... today.	**hoy.** oy
... yesterday.	**ayer.** ah·*yehr*
... on Monday.	**el lunes.** el *loo*·nes

For days of the week, see p. 124.

It is defective.	**No está bien.** no eh·*stah* bee·*en*
Look.	**Mire.** *mee*·reh
Here. [*point*]	**Aquí.** ah·*kee*

Can you ...	**¿Puede...**
	pweh·deh
... exchange it?	**cambiarlo?**
	cahm·byar·lo
... give me a refund?	**devolverme el dinero?**
	dehbol·behr·meh el dee·neh·ro
... repair it?	**arreglarlo?**
	arreh·glar·lo
Here is the receipt.	**Aquí está el recibo.**
	ah·kee eh·stah el reh·thee·bo
Can I see the manager?	**¿Puedo ver al director?**
	pweh·do behr ahl direc·tor

Loss

See also "Theft" below. The lists are interchangeable.

I have lost ...	**He perdido...**
	eh pehr·dee·do
... my bracelet.	**mi pulsera.**
	mee pool·seh·rah
... my camera.	**mi cámara.**
	mee cah·mah·rah
... my car keys.	**las llaves de mi coche.**
	las yah·behs deh mee co·cheh
... my car registration.	**mi cartilla de propiedad.**
	mee car·tee·yah deh pro·pyeh·dahd
... my driver's license.	**mi carné de conducir.**
	mee car·neh deh condoo·theer
... my insurance certificate.	**mi certificado de seguro.**
	mee thehr·tifi·cah·do del seh·goo·ro
... my jewelry.	**mis joyas.**
	mees hoy·ahs
... my purse.	**mi bolso.**
	mee bol·so
... everything.	**todo.**
	to·do

Theft

See also "Loss" above. The lists are interchangeable.

Someone has stolen ...	**Alguien ha robado...**
	ahl·gyen ah ro·bah·do
... my car.	**mi coche.**
	mee co·cheh

Someone has stolen …	**Alguien ha robado…**
	ahl·*gyen* ah ro·*bah*·do
… my car radio.	**la radio de mi coche.**
	la *rah*·dyo deh mee *co*·cheh
… my keys.	**mis llaves.**
	mees *yah*·behs
… my luggage.	**mi equipaje.**
	mee ehkee·*pah*·heh
… my money.	**mi dinero.**
	mee dee·*neh*·ro
… my necklace.	**mi collar.**
	mee co·*yar*
… my passport.	**mi pasaporte.**
	mee pahsah·*por*·teh
… my radio.	**mi radio.**
	mee *rah*·dyo
… my tickets.	**mis billetes.**
	mees bee·*yeh*·tes
… my traveler's checks.	**mis cheques de viaje.**
	mees *cheh*·kes deh bee·*ah*·heh
… my wallet.	**mi cartera.**
	mee car·*teh*·rah
… my watch.	**mi reloj.**
	mee reh·*lo*

Likely Reactions

Wait.	**Espere.**
	eh·*speh*·reh
When?	**¿Cuándo?**
	cwahn·do
Where?	**¿Dónde?**
	don·deh
Your name?	**¿Nombre?**
	nom·breh
Address?	**¿Dirección?**
	direc·*thyon*
I can't help you.	**No puedo ayudarle.**
	no *pweh*·do ah·yoo·*dar*·leh
I can't do anything about it.	**Yo no tengo nada que ver.**
	yo no *ten*·go *nah*·dah keh behr

The Post Office

Essential Information

- For finding a post office, see p. 9.
- Here are signs to look for.

  Correos
  Correos y Telégrafos
  Servicio Postal

- It is best to buy stamps at a tobacco shop. Go to the post office only for more complicated transactions, such as sending a telegram. For signs indicating that stamps are sold, look for the words **sellos**, **timbres**, or **franqueos**.

- Look for a red and yellow sign on the shop.
- Letter boxes (**buzones**) are yellow. Mail all overseas correspondence in the slot marked **extranjero** or **otros destinos**.
- To have your mail "held," you will need to show your passport at the counter marked **Lista de Correos** in the main post office; you will pay a small charge.

What to Say

To the United States, please. [hand letters, cards, or parcels over the counter]	**Para los Estados Unidos, por favor.** pah·rah los eh·stah·dos oo·nee·dos por fah·bor
To Australia.	**Para Australia.** pah·rah ah·oo·strah·lyah
To England.	**Para Inglaterra.** pah·rah inglah·teh·rah

For names of countries, see p. 128.

How much is …	**¿Cuánto es…** cwahn·to es
… this parcel (to Canada)?	**este paquete (para Canadá)?** eh·steh pah·keh·teh (pah·rah cahnah·dah)
… a letter (to Australia)?	**una carta (para Australia)?** oo·nah car·tah (pah·rah ah·oo·strah·lyah)

How much is …

¿Cuánto es…
cwahn·to es

… a postcard (to the United States)?

una postal (para los Estados Unidos)?
oo·nah po·stahl (pah·rah los eh·stah·dos oo·nee·dos)

Airmail.

Por avión.
por ah·byon

Surface mail.

Por correo ordinario.
por co·rreh·o ordee·nah·reeo

One stamp, please.

Un sello, por favor.
oon seh·yo por fah·bor

Two stamps.

Dos sellos.
dos seh·yos

A (one-euro) stamp.

Un sello (de un euro).
oon seh·yo (deh oon eh·ooro)

A (15-cent) stamp.

Un sello (de quince céntimos).
oon seh·yo (deh keen·theh then·teemos)

I would like to send a telegram.

Quiero enviar un telegrama.
kee·eh·ro enbee·ar oon tehleh·grah·mah

Telephoning

Essential Information

- In Spain, public telephones (**cabinas telefónicas**) are bright green, marked with the word **Teléfonos**. Insert at least 20 céntimos for a local call and 50 céntimos for calls to another province.

- For international calls, it is easier to use newer phones that take international calling cards, which are available at tobacco shops. If you use an international calling card, dial the access number on the back of the card. You will be prompted to dial the PIN number for the card, then the number you want to reach.

- Alternatively, dial the appropriate access number for AT&T, MCI, or Sprint, and you can have the charges applied to a credit card.

- In large cities, many public telephones have been replaced by **locutorios**, which are call centers with special international calling rates.

- To call the United States, dial the country code 1, then the area code and number you want to call. Canada's country code is also 1.

- For calls to countries that cannot be dialed direct or if you have difficulties in placing a call, go to the **Central Telefónica** (**CTNE**) or **Teléfonos**, which are open 24 hours a day in large towns. In **la Telefónica**, the operator will put your call through and give you the bill afterwards. Just write the name of the town and the telephone number you want to reach on a piece of paper, and hand it to the operator. Add **de persona a persona** if you want a person-to-person call or **a cobro revertido** if you want to call collect.

- In Mexico, you should look for public telephones marked **TELMEX** for the most reasonably priced access to international long distance service. Purchase an international calling card for the best long distance rates; these are available at small shops and newsstands.

- For calls within Mexico, purchase a debit card for use at **LADATEL** public telephones. Be aware that international calls from **LADATEL** public telephones can be quite expensive. **LADATEL** cards are available at small shops and newsstands.

- To ask the way to a public telephone, see p. 12.

What to Say

Where can I make a telephone call?	**¿Dónde puedo llamar por teléfono?**
	don·deh *pweh*·do yah·*mar* por teh·*leh*·fono
Local/long distance.	**Local/al extranjero.**
	lo·*cahl*/al extrahn·*heh*·ro
I'd like this number ... [*show number*]	**Quiero este número...**
	kee·*eh*·ro *eh*·steh *noo*·mehro
... in the United States.	**en los Estados Unidos.**
	en los eh·*stah*·dos oo·*nee*·dos
... in Canada.	**en Canadá.**
	en cahnah·*dah*

For the names of other countries, see p. 128.

Can you dial it for me, please?	**¿Puede usted marcar por mí, por favor?**
	pweh·deh oo·*sted* mar·*car* por mee por fah·*bor*
How much is it?	**¿Cuánto es?**
	cwahn·to es
Hello!	**¡Hola!**
	o·lah
May I speak to _____ ?	**¿Puedo hablar con _____ ?**
	pweh·do ah·*blar* con...
Extension _____ .	**Extensión _____ .**
	exten·*syon*...
I'm sorry, I don't speak Spanish.	**Lo siento, no hablo español.**
	lo see·*en*·to no *hah*·blo espah·*nyol*
Do you speak English?	**¿Habla usted inglés?**
	ah·blah oo·*sted* in·*glehs*
Thank you, I'll call back.	**Gracias, volveré a llamar.**
	grah·thyahs bolbeh·*reh* ah yah·*mar*
Good-bye.	**Adiós.**
	ah·*dyos*

Likely Reactions

That's 80 cents.	**Son ochenta céntimos.**
	son o·*chen*·tah *then*·timos
Booth number (3).	**Cabina número (tres).**
	cah·*bee*·nah *noo*·meh·ro (tres)

For numbers, see p. 120.

Don't hang up.	**No cuelgue.** no *cwehl*·geh
I am trying to connect you.	**Estoy intentando comunicarle.** eh·*stoy* inten·*tahn*·do comooni·*car*·leh
Go ahead; you're connected.	**Hable.** *ah*·bleh
There's a delay.	**Hay retraso.** *ah*·ee reh·*trah*·so
I'll try again.	**Probaré otra vez.** probah·*reh* o·trah behth

Cashing Checks and Changing Money

Essential Information

- To ask directions to a bank or currency exchange office, see p. 10.
- Look for the following words to find places for banking.

Banco	Bank
Caja de Ahorros	Savings bank
Caja de Cambio	Currency exchange desk in a bank
Oficina de Cambio	Currency exchange office

- You may access funds from your United States bank at most ATMs by using your ATM card. You may also cash traveler's checks at any bank displaying the Eurocheque sign.
- Have your passport handy, and remember that in Spain banks open at 9 A.M. and close at 2 P.M., except on Saturdays, when they close at 1 P.M.

What to Say

I'd like to cash …	**Quiero cobrar…**
	kee·*eh*·ro co·*brar*
… this traveler's check.	**este cheque de viaje.**
	eh·steh *cheh*·keh deh bee·*ah*·heh
… these traveler's checks.	**estos cheques de viaje.**
	eh·stos *cheh*·kes deh bee·*ah*·heh
… this check.	**este cheque.**
	eh·steh *cheh*·keh
I'd like to change this into euros.	**Quiero cambiar esto en euros.**
	kee·*eh*·ro cahm·*byar* *eh*·sto en *eh*·ooros
Here is …	**Aquí está…**
	ah·*kee* eh·*stah*
… my ATM card.	**mi tarjeta de banco.**
	mee tar·*heh*·tah deh *bahn*·co
… my passport.	**mi pasaporte.**
	mee pahsah·*por*·teh
What is the exchange rate?	**¿A cuánto está el cambio?**
	ah *cwahn*·to eh·*stah* el *cahm*·byo

Likely Reactions

Passport, please.

Pasaporte, por favor.
  pahsah·*por*·teh por fah·*bor*

Sign here.

Firme aquí.
  feer·meh ah·*kee*

Your ATM card, please.

Su tarjeta de banco, por favor.
  soo tar·*heh*·tah deh *bahn*·co
  por fah·*bor*

Go to the cashier's window.

Vaya a caja.
  bah·yah ah *cah*·hah

Automobile Travel

Essential Information

- To ask directions to a gas station or garage, see p. 11.
- Look for the following signs.

Gasolina	Gasoline
Gasolinera	Gas station
Estación de servicio	Gas station

- There are four grades of gasoline.

Normal	Regular
Súper	Plus
Extra	Super/premium
Gas-oil	Diesel

- One gallon is approximately 3¾ liters (accurate enough up to 6 gallons).
- Gasoline prices are standardized throughout Spain, and a minimum sale of 5 liters is often imposed.
- For car repairs, look for signs with red, blue, and white stripes, or look for the following signs.

Garaje
Taller de reparaciones

- Most gas stations offer 24-hour service, although some close late at night. Take care, however, because stations are few and far between.
- There are emergency telephones located at intervals along all major highways where you can contact **Asistencia en Carretera** (Road Assistance) in the event of an accident or emergency.
- For road signs and warnings, see p. 115.

What to Say

For numbers, see p. 120.

(Nine) liters of …	**(Nueve) litros de…** (*nweh*·beh) *lee*·tros deh
(Ten) euros of …	**(Diez) euros de…** (dee·*eth*) eh·ooros deh
… regular.	**normal.** nor·*mahl*

(Nine) liters of …	**(Nueve) litros de…** (*nweh*·beh) *lee*·tros deh
(Ten) euros of …	**(Diez) euros de…** (dee·*eth*) eh·ooros deh
… plus.	**súper.** *soo*·pehr
… premium.	**extra.** *ex*·trah
… diesel.	**gas-oil.** gahs·oyl
Fill it up, please.	**Lleno, por favor.** *yeh*·no por fah·*bor*
Will you check …	**¿Puede mirar…** *pweh*·deh mee·*rar*
… the battery?	**la batería?** la bahteh·*ree*·ah
… the oil?	**el aceite?** el ah·*thay*·teh
… the radiator?	**el radiador?** el rahdyah·*dor*
… the tires?	**los neumáticos?** los neh·oo·*mah*·ticos
I have run out of gasoline.	**Me he quedado sin gasolina.** meh eh keh·*dah*·do sin gahso·*lee*·nah
Can I borrow a can, please?	**¿Puede dejarme una lata, por favor?** *pweh*·deh deh·*har*·meh *oo*·nah *lah*·tah por fah·*bor*
My car has broken down.	**Se ha averiado mi coche.** seh ah ahbehree·*ah*·do mee *co*·cheh
My car won't start.	**Mi coche no arranca.** mee *co*·cheh no ah·*rrahn*·cah
I have had an accident.	**He tenido un accidente.** eh teh·*nee*·do oon ahcthee·*den*·teh
I have lost my car keys.	**He perdido las llaves de mi coche.** eh pehr·*dee*·do las *yah*·behs deh mee *co*·cheh
My car is …	**Mi coche está…** mee *co*·cheh eh·*stah*
… two kilometers away.	**a dos kilómetros.** ah dos ki·*lo*·mehtros

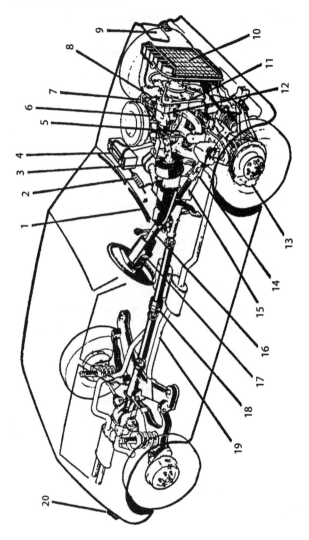

1 windshield wipers
limpiaparabrisas
limpyah-pahrah-*bree*-sahs

2 fuses
fusibles
foo-*see*-bles

3 heater
calentador
cahlentah-*dor*

4 battery
batería
bahteh-*ree*-ah

5 engine
motor
mo-*tor*

6 fuel pump
bomba de gasolina
bom-bah deh gahso-*lee*-nah

7 starter
motor de arranque
mo-*tor* deh ah-*rrahn*-keh

8 carburetor
carburador
carboorah-*dor*

9 headlights
faros
fah-ros

10 radiator
radiador
rahdyah-*dor*

11 fan belt
correa del ventilador
co-*rreh*-ah del benteelah-*dor*

12 alternator
generador
heh-nehrah-*dor*

13 brakes
frenos
freh-nos

14 clutch
embrague
em-*brah*-gueh

15 gear box
caja de cambios
cah-hah deh *cahm*-byos

16 steering
dirección
direc-*thyon*

17 ignition
encendido
enthen-*dee*-do

18 transmission
transmisión
trahnsmee-*syon*

19 exhaust pipe
tubo de escape
too-bo deh eh-*scah*-peh

20 turn signals
indicadores
indeecah-*dor*-es

My car is …

Mi coche está…
mee *co*·cheh eh·*stah*

… three kilometers away.

a tres kilómetros.
ah tres ki·*lo*·mehtros

Can you help me, please?

¿Puede ayudarme, por favor?
pweh·deh ah·yoo·*dar*·meh por
fah·*bor*

Do you repair cars?

¿Hacen reparaciones?
ah·then rehpahrah·*thyo*·nes

I have a flat tire.

Tengo un neumático pinchado.
ten·go oon neh·oo·*mah*·tico
pin·*chah*·do

I have a broken windshield.

Tengo el parabrisas roto.
ten·go el pahrah·*bree*·sahs *ro*·to

I think the problem is here.
[*point*]

Creo que el problema está aquí.
creh·o keh el pro·*bleh*·mah eh·*stah*
ah·*kee*

I don't know what's wrong.

No sé lo que está mal.
no seh lo keh eh·*stah* mahl

Can you …

¿Puede…
pweh·deh

… repair it?

reparar la avería?
rehpah·*rar* la ahbeh·*ree*·ah

… come and look?

venir a ver?
beh·*neer* ah behr

… give me an estimate?

estimar el coste?
ehstee·*mar* el *co*·steh

… write it down?

escribirlo?
ehscri·*beer*·lo

Do you accept these coupons?

¿Aceptan estos cupones?
ah·*thep*·tahn eh·stos coo·*po*·nes

How long will it take to
repair it?

**¿Cuánto tiempo tardarán en
repararlo?**
cwahn·to tee·*em*·po tardah·*rahn* en
rehpah·*rar*·lo

When will the car be ready?

¿Cuándo estará listo el coche?
cwahn·do ehstah·*rah* lee·sto el
co·cheh

Can I see the bill?

¿Puedo ver la cuenta?
pweh·do behr la *cwehn*·tah

This is my insurance
information.

Este es mi documento del seguro.
eh·steh es mee docoo·*men*·to del
seh·*goo*·ro

Renting a Car

Can I rent a car?	**¿Puedo alquilar un coche?** *pweh*·do ahlkee·*lar* oon *co*·cheh
I need a car …	**Necesito un coche…** neh·theh·*see*·to oon *co*·cheh
… for two people …	**para dos personas** *pah*·rah dos pehr·*so*·nahs
… for five people …	**para cinco personas** *pah*·rah *theen*·co pehr·*so*·nahs
… for one day.	**para un día.** *pah*·rah oon *dee*·ah
… for five days.	**para cinco días.** *pah*·rah *theen*·co *dee*·ahs
… for a week.	**para una semana.** *pah*·rah *oo*·nah seh·*mah*·nah
Can you write down …	**¿Puede escribir…** *pweh*·deh ehscri·*beer*
… the deposit to pay?	**el depósito de pago?** el deh·*po*·sito deh *pah*·go
… the charge per kilometer?	**el precio por kilómetro?** el *preh*·thyo por ki·*lo*·mehtro
… the daily charge?	**el precio por día?** el *preh*·thyo por *dee*·ah
… the cost of insurance?	**el precio del seguro?** el *preh*·thyo del seh·*goo*·ro
Can I leave it in (Madrid)?	**¿Puedo dejarlo en (Madrid)?** *pweh*·do deh·*har*·lo en (mah·*dreed*)
What documents do I need?	**¿Qué documentos necesito?** keh docoo·*men*·tos neh·theh·*see*·to

Likely Reactions

We don't do repairs.	**No se hacen reparaciones.** no seh *ah*·then rehpahrah·*thyo*·nes
Where is your car?	**¿Dónde está su coche?** *don*·deh eh·*stah* soo *co*·cheh
What make is it?	**¿Qué tipo es?** keh *tee*·po es
Come back tomorrow/ on Monday.	**Vuelva mañana/el lunes.** *bwel*·bah mahn·*yah*·nah/el *loo*·nes

For days of the week, see p. 124.

We don't rent cars.	**No se alquilan coches.** no seh ahl·*kee*·lahn *co*·ches

Your driver's license, please.

Su carné de conducir, por favor.
soo car·*neh* deh condoo·*theer* por
fah·*bor*

The mileage is unlimited.

El kilometraje es ilimitado.
el kilomeh·*trah*·heh es
ileemee·*tah*·do

Public Transportation

Essential Information

- To ask directions to a bus stop, the bus station, the train station, or a taxi stand, see pp. 10–12.

- Taxis are usually white sedans with a colored line painted along the side. If a taxi is available, during the day it displays a sign on the windshield that says **libre** (free) and at night it displays a green light.

- Here are the different types of trains, listed according to speed (slowest to fastest).

Expreso/Rápido	Do not be misled by their names; these are both slow trains, the only difference being the first travels by night, the second by day.
TALGO	Luxury train
AVE	High-speed luxury train that connects Madrid to several other large towns, more expensive
Regional	Trains, operating within specific regions, which make many local stops
Cercanías	Commuter trains that connect large cities, like Madrid and Barcelona

- Here are the signs to look for. (See also p. 115.)

Andén	Platform
Billetes	Tickets, ticket booth
Consigna/equipajes	Luggage storage
Despacho de billetes/taquilla	Ticket booth
Entrada	Entrance
Horario	Schedule
Llegada	Arrival
Oficina de Información	Information office
Parada	Bus stop, taxi stand
Prohibido	Prohibited
RENFE	Initials of Spanish railway
Salida	Exit

- Children travel free up to the age of three, and they pay half price up to the age of seven. However, if you have an international ticket, children can travel free up to the age of four and half price up to the age of twelve.

- On certain dates throughout the year known as **Días Azules** (Blue Days), many reductions are available on train travel; check with the Spanish Tourist Office for dates and further information.

- On buses and subways there is a flat rate regardless of distance. It is cheaper to buy a **taco** (book of tickets) for subway travel. Subways operate between 6 A.M. and 1 A.M.

- It is worthwhile to purchase train and bus tickets in advance.

What to Say

Where does the train for (Madrid) leave from?

¿De dónde sale el tren para (Madrid)?
deh *don*·deh *sah*·leh el tren *pah*·rah (ma·*dreed*)

(At) what time does the train leave for (Madrid)?

¿A qué hora sale el tren para (Madrid)?
ah keh *o*·rah *sah*·leh el tren *pah*·rah (ma·*dreed*)

(At) what time does the train arrive in (Madrid)?

¿A qué hora llega el tren a (Madrid)?
ah keh *o*·rah *yeh*·gah el tren a (ma·*dreed*)

Is this the train for (Madrid)?

¿Es éste el tren para (Madrid)?
es *eh*·steh el tren *pah*·rah (ma·*dreed*)

Where does the bus for (Barcelona) leave from?

¿De dónde sale el autobús para (Barcelona)?
deh *don*·deh *sah*·leh el ah·ooto·*boos pah*·rah (bartheh·*lo*·nah)

(At) what time does the bus arrive at (Barcelona)?

¿A qué hora llega el autobús (Barcelona)?
ah keh *o*·rah *yeh*·gah el ah·ooto·*boos* a (bartheh·*lo*·nah)

Is this the bus for (Barcelona)?

¿Es éste el autobús para (Barcelona)?
es *eh*·steh el ah·ooto·*boos pah*·rah (bartheh·*lo*·nah)

Do I have to change (trains)?	**¿Tengo que cambiar?** *ten*·go keh cahm·*byar*
Where does … leave from?	**¿De dónde sale…** deh *don*·deh sah·leh
… the bus …	**el autobús** el ah·ooto·*boos*
… the boat/ferry …	**el barco/ferry** el *bar*·co/*feh*·rree
… the subway …	**el metro** el *meh*·tro
… the train …	**el tren** el tren
… for the airport …	**para el aeropuerto?** *pah*·rah el ah·ehro·*pwehr*·to
… for the cathedral …	**para la catedral?** *pah*·rah la cahteh·*drahl*
… for the beach …	**para la playa?** *pah*·rah la *plah*·yah
… for the marketplace …	**para el mercado?** *pah*·rah el mehr·*cah*·do
… for the train station …	**para la estación de tren?** *pah*·rah la ehstah·*thyon* deh tren
… for the center of town …	**para el centro de la ciudad?** *pah*·rah el *then*·tro deh la theeoo·*dahd*
… for the town hall …	**para el ayuntamiento?** *pah*·rah el ah·yoontah·*myen*·to
… for (St. John's) Church …	**para la iglesia (de San Juan)?** *pah*·rah la ee·*gleh*·syah (deh sahn hwahn)
… for the swimming pool …	**para la piscina?** *pah*·rah la pis·*thee*·nah
Is this …	**¿Es éste…** es *eh*·steh
… the bus to the marketplace?	**el autobús para el mercado?** el ah·ooto·*boos pah*·rah el mehr·*cah*·do
… the bus to the train station?	**el autobús para la estación de tren?** el ah·ooto·*boos pah*·rah la ehstah·*thyon* deh tren
Where can I get a taxi?	**¿Dónde puedo tomar un taxi?** *don*·deh *pweh*·do to·*mar* oon *tahx*·ee

Can you tell me when to get off, please?
¿Puede avisarme en mi parada, por favor?
pweh·deh ahbee·sar·meh en mee pah·rah·dah por fah·bor

Can I reserve a seat?
¿Puedo reservar un asiento?
pweh·do rehsehr·bar oon ah·syen·to

A one-way ticket.
Un billete de ida solamente.
oon bee·yeh·teh deh ee·dah solah·men·teh

A round-trip ticket.
Un billete de ida y vuelta.
oon bee·yeh·teh deh ee·dah ee bwel·tah

First class.
Primera clase.
pree·meh·rah clah·seh

Second class.
Segunda clase.
seh·goon·dah clah·seh

One adult …
Un adulto…
oon ah·dool·to

Two adults …
Dos adultos…
dos ah·dool·tos

… and one child.
y un niño.
ee oon neen·yo

… and two children.
y dos niños.
y dos neen·yos

How much is it?
¿Cuánto es?
cwahn·to es

Likely Reactions

Over there.
Allí.
ah·yee

Here.
Aquí.
ah·kee

Platform (1).
Andén (primero).
ahn·den (pree·meh·ro)

At (four o'clock).
A las (cuatro).
ah las (cwah·tro)

For telling time, see p. 122.

Change at (Zaragoza).
Cambie en (Zaragoza).
cahm·byeh en (thah·rah·go·thah)

Change at (the town hall).
Cambie en (el ayuntamiento).
cahm·byeh en (el ah·yoontah·myen·to)

This is your stop.	**Esta es su parada.**
	eh·stah es soo pah·*rah*·dah
There is only first class.	**Sólo hay primera clase.**
	so·lo *ah*·ee pree·*meh*·rah *clah*·seh

Leisure and Entertainment

Essential Information

- To ask directions to a place of entertainment, see pp. 10–12.
- For telling time, see p. 122.
- For important signs, see p. 115.
- It is common for shows, movies, or plays to have a late night session that ends at 1 A.M.–2 A.M.
- Smoking is strictly forbidden in movies and theaters.
- Theater ushers should be tipped.
- Most movie and theater seats can be reserved in advance, either by phone or on the Internet.
- In bars, cafés, and restaurants it is customary to leave a tip, even if you drink at the bar. You pay when you leave.

What to Say

(At) what time does … open?	**¿A qué hora abre…** ah keh o·rah *ah*·breh
(At) what time does … close?	**¿A qué hora cierra…** ah keh o·rah thee·*eh*·rrah
… the art gallery …	**la galería de arte?** la gahleh·*ree*·ah deh *ar*·teh
… the botanical garden …	**el jardín botánico?** el har·*deen* bo·*tah*·nico
… the cinema …	**el cine?** el *thee*·neh
… the concert hall …	**la sala de conciertos?** la *sah*·lah deh con·*thyehr*·tos
… the disco …	**la discoteca?** la disco·*teh*·cah
… the museum …	**el museo?** el moo·*seh*·o
… the nightclub …	**la sala de fiestas?** la *sah*·lah deh fee·*eh*·stahs
… the sports stadium …	**el estadio de deportes?** el eh·*stah*·dyo deh deh·*por*·tes
… the swimming pool …	**la piscina?** la pis·*thee*·nah

(At) what time does … open?	**¿A qué hora abre…** ah keh *o*·rah *ah*·breh
(At) what time does … close?	**¿A qué hora cierra…** ah keh *o*·rah thee·*eh*·rrah
… the theater …	**el teatro?** el teh·*ah*·tro
… the zoo …	**el zoo?** el *tho*·o
(At) what time does … start?	**¿A qué hora empieza…** ah keh *o*·rah em·*pyeh*·thah
… the cabaret …	**el cabaret?** el cahbah·*reh*
… the concert …	**el concierto?** el con·*thyehr*·to
… the game/match …	**el partido?** el par·*tee*·do
… the movie …	**la película?** la peh·*lee*·coolah
… the play …	**la obra?** la *o*·brah
… the race …	**la carrera?** la cah·*rreh*·rah
How much is it …	**¿Cuánto es…** *cwahn*·to es
… for an adult?	**por un adulto?** por oon ah·*dool*·to
… for a child?	**por un niño?** por oon *nee*·nyo
Stalls/circle/sun/shade [*state the price, if there's a choice*]	**Butaca/anfiteatro/sol/sombra** boo·*tah*·cah/ahnfeeteh·*ah*·tro/ sol/*som*·brah
Do you have …	**¿Tiene…** tee·*en*·eh
… a guidebook?	**una guía?** *oo*·nah *ghee*·ah
… a program?	**un programa?** oon pro·*grah*·mah
Where is the restroom, please?	**¿Dónde están los servicios, por favor?** *don*·deh eh·*stahn* los sehr·*bee*·thyos por fah·*bor*
Where is the coatroom?	**¿Dónde está el guardarropa?** *don*·deh eh·*stah* el gwardah·*rro*·pah

I would like lessons in …	**Quiero lecciones de…**
	kee·*eh*·ro lec·*thyo*·nes deh
… sailing.	**vela.**
	beh·lah
… scuba diving.	**buceo.**
	boo·*theh*·o
… skiing.	**esquí.**
	eh·*skee*
… water skiing.	**esquí acuático.**
	eh·*skee* ah·*cwah*·tico
Can I rent …	**¿Puedo alquilar…**
	pweh·do ahlkee·*lar*
… a beach umbrella?	**una sombrilla?**
	oo·nah som·*bree*·yah
… a boat?	**un bote?**
	oon *bo*·teh
… a deckchair?	**una hamaca?**
	oo·nah ah·*mah*·cah
… a fishing rod?	**una caña de pescar?**
	oo·nah *cah*·nyah deh peh·*scar*
… some skis?	**unos esquís?**
	oo·nos eh·*skees*
… some ski boots?	**unas botas de esquí?**
	oo·nahs *bo*·tahs deh eh·*skee*
… the necessary equipment?	**el equipo necesario?**
	el eh·*kee*·po neh·theh·*sah*·reeo
How much is it …	**¿Cuánto es…**
	cwahn·to es
… per day/per hour?	**por día/por hora?**
	por *dee*·ah/por *o*·rah
Do I need a license?	**¿Necesito licencia?**
	neh·theh·*see*·to lee·*then*·thyah

Asking If Things Are Allowed

Essential Information

- The following questions can all be asked in one way in Spanish:
  ¿Se puede fumar aquí?

  May one smoke here?
  May I smoke here?
  May we smoke here?
  Can one smoke here?
  Can I smoke here?
  Can we smoke here?
  Is it okay to smoke here?

- To save space, only the first English version ("May one ...?") is given below.

What to Say

Excuse me, please.	**Perdone, por favor.** pehr·*do*·neh por fah·*bor*
May one ...	**¿Se puede...** seh *pweh*·deh
... camp here?	**acampar aquí?** ahcahm·*par* ah·*kee*
... come in?	**entrar?** en·*trar*
... dance here?	**bailar aquí?** bah·ee·*lar* ah·*kee*
... fish here?	**pescar aquí?** peh·*scar* ah·*kee*
... get a drink here?	**obtener una bebida aquí?** obteh·*nehr* oo·nah beh·*bee*·dah ah·*kee*
... get out this way?	**salir por aquí?** sah·*leer* por ah·*kee*
... get something to eat here?	**obtener algo de comer aquí?** obteh·*nehr ahl*·go deh co·*mehr* ah·*kee*
... leave one's things here?	**dejar las cosas aquí?** deh·*har* las *co*·sahs ah·*kee*
... look around?	**mirar esto?** mee·*rar* eh·sto

May one …	**¿Se puede…** seh *pweh*·deh
… make a telephone call here?	**telefonear aquí?** telefoneh·*ar* ah·*kee*
… park here?	**aparcar aquí?** ahpar·*car* ah·*kee*
… picnic here?	**comer aquí?** co·*mehr* ah·*kee*
… sit here?	**sentar aquí?** sen·*tar* ah·*kee*
… smoke here?	**fumar aquí?** foo·*mar* ah·*kee*
… swim here?	**nadar aquí?** nah·*dar* ah·*kee*
… take photos here?	**tomar fotos aquí?** to·*mar* fo·tos ah·*kee*
… wait here?	**esperar aquí?** ehspeh·*rar* ah·*kee*

Likely Reactions

Yes, certainly.	**Sí, desde luego.** see *des*·deh *lweh*·go
Help yourself.	**Sírvase usted mismo.** *seer*·bahseh oo·*sted* mees·mo
I think so.	**Creo que sí.** *creh*·o keh see
Of course.	**Claro.** *clah*·ro
Yes, but be careful.	**Sí, pero tenga cuidado.** see *peh*·ro ten·gah cwee·*dah*·do
No, certainly not.	**No, desde luego que no.** no *des*·deh *lweh*·go keh no
I don't think so.	**No creo.** no *creh*·o
Not normally.	**Normalmente no.** normal·*men*·teh no
Sorry.	**Lo siento.** lo see·*en*·to

Reference

Public Notices

Signs for Drivers, Pedestrians, Travelers, Shoppers, and Overnight Guests

Abierto	Open
Aduana	Customs
Agua potable	Drinking water
Alquiler de coches	Cars for rent
Alto	Stop
Andén	Platform, track [*railway*]
Aparcamiento	Parking lot
Ascensor	Elevator
Aseos	Restrooms
Atención al tren	Caution: Trains
Autobús solamente	For buses (only)
Autopista	Highway
Autoservicio	Self-service
Badén permanente	No parking (in constant use)
Bar	Bar
Baños	Baths/bathrooms
Caballeros	Gentlemen
Caja	Teller, cashier
Caliente	Hot (water)
Calzada deteriorada	Uneven surface
Callejón sin salida	Dead end street
Camino cerrado	Road closed
Cañada	Cattle crossing
Caza	Hunting
Ceda el paso	Yield
Centro ciudad	Town center
Cerrado	Closed
Cerrado por vacaciones	Closed for vacation
Circulación en ambas direcciones	Two-way traffic
Circulen por la derecha	Keep right
Coche restaurante	Dining car
Comedor	Dining room
Completo	No vacancies
Conserje	Porter
Consigna	Luggage storage

Cruce	Crossroad, intersection
Cruce de ciclistas	Bicycle crossing
Cuidado	Watch out
Cuidado con el perro	Beware of the dog
Curva peligrosa	Dangerous curve [*in road*]
Damas	Ladies
Despacio	Drive slowly
Despacho de billetes	Ticket booth
Desprendimiento del terreno	Falling rocks
Desvío	Detour
Dirección única	One-way (street)
Disco obligatorio	Parking tokens required
Ducha	Shower
Empuje	Push
Encienda los faros	Turn lights on
Entrada	Entrance
Entrada libre	Free admission/entrance
Entre sin llamar	Enter without knocking
Es peligroso asomarse al exterior	It's dangerous to lean out of the window
Escalera automática	Escalator
Escuela	School
Espere	Wait
Estacionamiento limitado	Restricted parking
Estrechamiento de calzada	Road narrows
Final de autopista	End (of highway)
Firme (superficie) deslizante	Slippery surface [*road*]
Frío	Cold
Guía	Guide(book)
Horas de visita	Visiting hours
Información	Information office/desk
Lavabos	Restrooms
Liquidación	Sale
Llame a la puerta	Knock (at the door)
Llegadas	Arrivals
Mayores	Adults
Metro	Subway
Niños	Children
No hay entradas (localidades)	Full house (movie, theater, etc.)
No potable	Not for drinking

No se admiten caravanas	No trailers
No tocar	Do not touch
Objetos perdidos	Lost and found
Obras	Construction
Ocupado	Occupied
Oferta especial	Special offer
Ojo al tren	Caution: Trains
Parada	Stop
Pasen	Cross (the road)
Paso a nivel	Level crossing
Paso subterráneo	Underground crossing
Peaje	Toll
Peatón, circula por tu izquierda	Pedestrians keep to the left
Peatones	Pedestrians
Peligro	Danger
Peligro de incendio	Danger of fire
Pesca	Fishing
Piso (primero, segundo, tercero, planta baja, sótano)	Floor (first, second, third, ground, basement)
Plazas libres	Vacancy
Policía	Police
Precaución	Caution
Precios fijos	Fixed prices
Principio de autopista	Start (of highway)
Prioridad a la derecha	Right of way (on the right)
Privado	Private
Prohibido	Forbidden
Prohibido adelantar	No passing
Prohibido aparcar	No parking
Prohibido bañarse sin gorro	No bathing without a cap
Prohibido el paso	Trespassers will be prosecuted
Prohibido fumar	No smoking
Prohibido hablar al conductor	No talking to the driver
Prohibido pisar el césped	Keep off the grass
Prohibido tomar fotografías	No photographs
Rebajas	Sales
Recién pintado	Wet paint
Recepción	Reception
Reduzca velocidad	Slow down
Reservado	Reserved

Reservas	Reservations
Retrete	Toilet
Sala de espera	Waiting room
Saldos	Sales, sale merchandise
Salida	Exit
Salida de emergencia	Emergency exit
Salidas	Departures
Se alquila habitación	Room for rent
Se prohíbe la entrada	No admission/no entrance
Se vende	For sale
Semáforo	Traffic light
Señoras	Ladies
Señores	Gentlemen
Servicios	Restrooms
Siga adelante	Go
Silencio	Quiet
Taquilla	Ticket booth
Vehículos pesados	For heavy vehicles
Velocidad limitada	Speed limit
Veneno	Poison
Venta	For sale
Ventanilla	Window (of ticket office)
Zona azul	Restricted parking
Zona de avalanchas	Avalanche area

Abbreviations

A	**Albergue**	inn/hostel
ANCE	**Agrupación Nacional de Campings de España**	Spanish Federation of Camping Sites
apdo	**apartado (de correos)**	post office box
Av/Avda	**Avenida**	avenue
C	**Carretera comarcal**	provincial road
	Caliente	hot (water faucet)
C/	**Calle**	street
	Cuenta	account
CAMPSA	**Compañía Arrendataria del Monopolio de Petróleos Sociedad Anónima**	national gasoline company
cént(s)	**céntimo(s)**	euro cent(s)
CN	**Carretera Nacional**	national road
CT	**Centro Turístico**	tourist center

dcha	**derecha**	right
dto	**descuento**	discount
F	**Frío**	cold (water faucet)
FC	**Ferrocarril**	railway
FEVE	**Ferrocarriles Españoles de Vía Estrecha**	Spanish railway company
GC	**Guardia Civil**	Civil Guard
h	**hora**	hour
	habitantes	inhabitants
	hacia	circa
IB	**Iberia**	Spanish airline
izq	**izquierdo**	left
km/h	**kilómetros por hora**	kilometers per hour
kv	**kilovatios**	kilowatts
L	**Carretera Local**	local road
MIT	**Ministerio de Información y Turismo**	Ministry of Tourism
N	**Nacional (carretera)**	national road
	norte	north
no.	**número**	number
num.	**número**	number
NO	**noroeste**	northwest
OP	**Obras Públicas**	public works
Pº	**Paseo**	avenue
PVP	**Precio de Venta al Público**	retail price
RACE	**Real Automóvil Club de España**	Royal Automobile Club of Spain
REAJ	**Red Española de Albergues Juveniles**	Youth Hostel Association
RENFE	**Red Nacional de Ferrocarriles Españoles**	Spanish national railway company
Sr	**Señor**	Mr.
Sra	**Señora**	Mrs.
Sres	**Senores**	Messrs.
SP	**Servicio Público**	public service (taxis and buses)
SR	**Sin Reserva**	without reservation
Tlfno	**Teléfono**	telephone
TVE	**Televisión Española**	Spanish television company
Vda de	**viuda de**	widow of
vg, vgr	**verbigracia**	namely

Numbers

Cardinal Numbers

0	**cero**	*theh*-ro
1	**uno**	*oo*-no
2	**dos**	dos
3	**tres**	tres
4	**cuatro**	*cwah*-tro
5	**cinco**	*theen*-co
6	**seis**	*seh*-is
7	**siete**	see-*eh*-teh
8	**ocho**	*o*-cho
9	**nueve**	*nweh*-beh
10	**diez**	dee-*eth*
11	**once**	*on*-theh
12	**doce**	*do*-theh
13	**trece**	*treh*-theh
14	**catorce**	cah-*tor*-theh
15	**quince**	*keen*-theh
16	**dieciséis**	dee-eth-ee-*seh*-is
17	**diecisiete**	dee-eth-ee-see-*eh*-teh
18	**dieciocho**	dee-eth-ee-*o*-cho
19	**diecinueve**	dee-eth-ee-*nweh*-beh
20	**veinte**	*bayn*-teh
21	**veintiuno**	bayntee-*oo*-no
22	**veintidós**	bayntee-*dos*
23	**veintitrés**	bayntee-*tres*
24	**veinticuatro**	bayntee-*cwah*-tro
25	**veinticinco**	bayntee-*theen*-co
26	**veintiséis**	bayntee-*seh*-is
27	**veintisiete**	bayntee-see-*eh*-teh
28	**veintiocho**	bayntee-*o*-cho
29	**veintinueve**	bayntee-*nweh*-beh
30	**treinta**	*trayn*-tah
31	**treinta y uno**	*trayn*-tah ee *oo*-no
35	**treinta y cinco**	*trayn*-tah ee *theen*-co
38	**treinta y ocho**	*trayn*-tah ee *o*-cho
40	**cuarenta**	cwah-*ren*-tah
41	**cuarenta y uno**	cwah-*ren*-tah ee *oo*-no
45	**cuarenta y cinco**	cwah-*ren*-tah ee *theen*-co
48	**cuarenta y ocho**	cwah-*ren*-tah ee *o*-cho
50	**cincuenta**	theen-*cwehn*-tah

55	**cincuenta y cinco**	theen-*cwehn*-tah ee *theen*-co
60	**sesenta**	seh-*sen*-tah
65	**sesenta y cinco**	seh-*sen*-tah ee *theen*-co
70	**setenta**	seh-*ten*-tah
75	**setenta y cinco**	seh-*ten*-tah ee *theen*-co
80	**ochenta**	o-*chen*-tah
85	**ochenta y cinco**	o-*chen*-tah ee *theen*-co
90	**noventa**	no-*ben*-tah
95	**noventa y cinco**	no-*ben*-tah ee *theen*-co
100	**cien**	thee-*en*
101	**ciento uno**	thee-*en*-to *oo*-no
102	**ciento dos**	thee-*en*-to dos
125	**ciento veinticinco**	thee-*en*-to bayntee-*theen*-co
150	**ciento cincuenta**	thee-*en*-to theen-*cwehn*-tah
175	**ciento setenta y cinco**	thee-*en*-to seh-*ten*-tah ee *theen*-co
200	**doscientos**	dos-thee-*en*-tos
300	**trescientos**	tres-thee-*en*-tos
400	**cuatrocientos**	cwahtro-thee-*en*-tos
500	**quinientos**	kee-*nyen*-tos
1000	**mil**	mil
1500	**mil quinientos**	mil kee-*nyen*-tos
2000	**dos mil**	dos mil
5000	**cinco mil**	*theen*-co mil
10,000	**diez mil**	dee-*eth* mil
100,000	**cien mil**	thee-*en* mil
1,000,000	**un millón**	oon mi-*yon*

Ordinal Numbers

1st	**primero (1º)**	pree-*meh*-ro
2nd	**segundo (2º)**	seh-*goon*-do
3rd	**tercero (3º)**	tehr-*theh*-ro
4th	**cuarto (4º)**	*cwahr*-to
5th	**quinto (5º)**	*keen*-to
6th	**sexto (6º)**	*sehx*-to
7th	**séptimo (7º)**	*sep*-teemo
8th	**octavo (8º)**	oc-*tah*-bo
9th	**noveno (9º)**	no-*beh*-no
10th	**décimo (10º)**	*deh*-theemo
11th	**undécimo (11º)**	un-*deh*-theemo
12th	**duodécimo (12º)**	doo-o-*deh*-theemo

Time

What time is it?	**¿Qué hora es?** keh *o*·rah es
It is one o'clock.	**Es la una.** es la *oo*·nah
It is …	**Son…** son
… two o'clock …	**las dos** las dos
… three o'clock …	**las tres** las tres
… four o'clock …	**las cuatro** las *cwah*·tro
… in the morning.	**de la mañana.** deh la mah·*nyah*·nah
… in the afternoon / in the evening.	**de la tarde.** deh la *tar*·deh
… at night.	**de la noche.** deh la *no*·cheh
It is …	**Es…** es
… noon.	**mediodía.** mehdyo·*dee*·ah
… midnight.	**medianoche.** mehdyah·*no*·cheh
It is …	**Son…** son
… five past five.	**las cinco y cinco.** las *theen*·co ee *theen*·co
… ten past five.	**las cinco y diez.** las *theen*·co ee dee·*eth*
… a quarter past five.	**las cinco y cuarto.** las *theen*·co ee *cwahr*·to
… twenty past five.	**las cinco y veinte.** las *theen*·co ee *bayn*·teh
… twenty-five past five.	**las cinco y veinticinco.** las *theen*·co ee bayntee·*theen*·co
… half past five.	**las cinco y media.** las *theen*·co ee *meh*·dyah
… twenty-five to six.	**las seis menos veinticinco.** las *seh*·is *meh*·nos bayntee·*theen*·co

It is …	**Son…**
	son
… twenty to six.	**las seis menos veinte.**
	las *seh*·is *meh*·nos *bayn*·teh
… a quarter to six.	**las seis menos cuarto.**
	las *seh*·is *meh*·nos *cwahr*·to
… ten to six.	**las seis menos diez.**
	las *seh*·is *meh*·nos dee·*eth*
… five to six.	**las seis menos cinco.**
	las *seh*·is *meh*·nos *theen*·co
(At) what time (does the train leave)?	**¿A qué hora sale el tren)?**
	ah keh *o*·rah (*sah*·leh el tren)
At …	**A las…**
	ah las
… 13:00.	**trece.**
	treh·theh
… 14:05.	**catorce cero cinco.**
	cah·*tor*·theh *theh*·ro *theen*·co
… 15:10.	**quince diez.**
	keen·theh dee·*eth*
… 16:15.	**dieciséis quince.**
	dee·eth·ee·*seh*·is *keen*·theh
… 17:20.	**diecisiete veinte.**
	dee·eth·ee·see·*eh*·teh *bayn*·teh
… 18:25.	**dieciocho veinticinco.**
	dee·eth·ee·*o*·cho bayn·tee·*theen*·co
… 19:30.	**diecinueve treinta.**
	dee·eth·ee·*nweh*·beh *trayn*·tah
… 20:35.	**veinte treinta y cinco.**
	bayn·teh *trayn*·tah ee *theen*·co
… 21:40.	**veintiuna cuarenta.**
	bayntee·*oo*·nah cwah·*ren*·tah
… 22:45.	**veintidós cuarenta y cinco.**
	bayntee·*dos* cwah·*ren*·tah ee *theen*·co
… 23:50.	**veintitrés cincuenta.**
	bayntee·*tres* theen·*cwehn*·tah
… 0:55.	**cero cincuenta y cinco.**
	theh·ro theen·*cwehn*·tah ee *theen*·co
In ten minutes.	**En diez minutos.**
	en dee·*eth* mee·*noo*·tos

In a quarter of an hour.	**En un cuarto de hora.** en oon *cwahr*·to deh *o*·rah
In half an hour.	**En media hora.** en *meh*·dyah *o*·rah
In three quarters of an hour.	**En tres cuartos de hora.** en tres *cwahr*·tos deh *o*·rah

Days

Monday	**lunes** *loo*·nes
Tuesday	**martes** *mar*·tes
Wednesday	**miércoles** mee·*ehr*·colehs
Thursday	**jueves** *hweh*·bes
Friday	**viernes** bee·*ehr*·nes
Saturday	**sábado** *sah*·bahdo
Sunday	**domingo** do·*meen*·go
last Monday	**el lunes pasado** el *loo*·nes pah·*sah*·do
next Tuesday	**el martes próximo** el *mar*·tes *prohx*·ee·mo
on Wednesday	**el miércoles** el mee·*ehr*·colehs
on Thursdays	**los jueves** los *hweh*·bes
until Friday	**hasta el viernes** *ah*·stah el bee·*ehr*·nes
before Saturday	**antes del sábado** *ahn*·tes del *sah*·bahdo
after Sunday	**después del domingo** deh·*spwehs* del do·*meen*·go
the day before yesterday	**anteayer** ahnteh·ah·*yehr*
two days ago	**hace dos días** *ah*·theh dos *dee*·ahs
yesterday	**ayer** ah·*yehr*

yesterday morning	**ayer por la mañana** ah·*yehr* por la mah·*nyah*·nah
yesterday afternoon	**ayer por la tarde** ah·*yehr* por la *tar*·deh
last night	**anoche** ah·*no*·cheh
today	**hoy** oy
this morning	**esta mañana** *eh*·stah mah·*nyah*·nah
this afternoon	**esta tarde** *eh*·stah *tar*·deh
tonight	**esta noche** *eh*·stah *no*·cheh
tomorrow	**mañana** mah·*nyah*·nah
tomorrow morning	**mañana por la mañana** mah·*nyah*·nah por la mah·*nyah*·nah
tomorrow afternoon/evening	**mañana por la tarde** mah·*nyah*·nah por la *tar*·deh
tomorrow night	**mañana por la noche** mah·*nyah*·nah por la *no*·cheh
the day after tomorrow	**pasado mañana** pah·*sah*·do mah·*nyah*·nah

Months, Dates, Seasons, and Years

January	**enero** eh·*neh*·ro
February	**febrero** feh·*breh*·ro
March	**marzo** *mar*·tho
April	**abril** ah·*breel*
May	**mayo** *mah*·yo
June	**junio** *hoo*·nyo
July	**julio** *hoo*·lyo
August	**agosto** ah·*go*·sto

September	**septiembre**
	sep·*tyem*·breh
October	**octubre**
	oc·*too*·breh
November	**noviembre**
	no·*byem*·breh
December	**diciembre**
	dee·*thyem*·breh
in January	**en enero**
	en eh·*neh*·ro
until February	**hasta febrero**
	ah·stah feh·*breh*·ro
before March	**antes de marzo**
	ahn·tes deh *mar*·tho
after April	**después de abril**
	deh·*spwehs* deh ah·*breel*
during May	**durante mayo**
	doo·*rahn*·teh *mah*·yo
not until June	**hasta junio no**
	ah·stah *hoo*·nyo no
the beginning of July	**principios de julio**
	prin·*thee*·pyos deh *hoo*·lyo
the middle of August	**mediados de agosto**
	meh·*dyah*·dos deh ah·*go*·sto
the end of September	**finales de septiembre**
	fee·*nah*·les deh sep·*tyem*·breh
last month	**el mes pasado**
	el mes pah·*sah*·do
this month	**este mes**
	eh·steh mes
next month	**el mes próximo**
	el mes *prohx*·ee·mo
in spring	**en primavera**
	en preemah·*beh*·rah
in summer	**en verano**
	en beh·*rah*·no
in autumn	**en otoño**
	en o·*to*·nyo
in winter	**en invierno**
	en in·*byehr*·no
this year	**este año**
	eh·steh *ah*·nyo

last year	**el año pasado**
	el *ah*·nyo pah·*sah*·do
next year	**el año próximo**
	el *ah*·nyo *prohx*·ee·mo
in 1995	**en mil novecientos noventa y cinco**
	en mil no·beh·thee·*en*·tos no·*ben*·tah ee *theen*·co
in 2000	**en el (año) dos mil**
	en el (*ah*·nyo) dos meel
in 2005	**en el (año) dos mil cinco**
	en el (*ah*·nyo) dos meel *theen*·co
What is the date today?	**¿Qué fecha es hoy?**
	keh *feh*·chah es oy
It is the 6th of March.	**Es el seis de marzo.**
	es el *seh*·is deh *mar*·tho
It is the 12th of April.	**Es el doce de abril.**
	es el *do*·theh deh ah·*breel*
It is the 21st of August.	**Es el veintiuno de agosto.**
	es el bayntee·*oo*·no deh ah·*go*·sto

Public Holidays

Banks, post offices, public offices, retail stores, and schools are closed on the following holidays.

January 1	**Año Nuevo**	New Year's Day
January 6	**Epifanía Día de Reyes**	Epiphany
March 19	**San José**	St. Joseph's Day
[*varies*]	**Jueves Santo**	Holy Thursday
[*varies*]	**Viernes Santo**	Good Friday
[*varies*]	**Día de la Ascensión**	Ascension Thursday
[*varies*]	**Corpus Christi**	Corpus Christi Day
May 1	**Día del Trabajo**	Labor Day
July 25	**Día de Santiago**	St. James' Day
August 15	**Día de la Asunción**	Assumption Day
October 12	**Día del Pilar**	Columbus Day
	Fiesta de la Hispanidad	
November 1	**Todos los Santos**	All Saints Day
December 8	**Inmaculada Concepción**	Immaculate Conception Day
December 25	**Navidad**	Christmas Day

Countries and Nationalities

Countries

Australia	**Australia** ah·oo·*strah*·lyah
Austria	**Austria** *ah*·oo·streeah
Belgium	**Bélgica** *behl*·hee·cah
Britain	**Gran Bretaña** gran breh·*tah*·nyah
Canada	**Canadá** cah·nah·*dah*
East Africa	**África del Este** *ah*·freecah del *eh*·steh
Eire	**Eire** *eh*·ireh
England	**Inglaterra** inglah·*teh*·rrah
France	**Francia** *frahn*·thyah
Germany	**Alemania** ahleh·*mah*·nyah
Greece	**Grecia** *greh*·thyah
India	**India** *in*·diah
Italy	**Italia** ee·*tahl*·yah
Luxembourg	**Luxemburgo** looxem·*boor*·go
Netherlands	**Los Países Bajos** los pah·*ee*·ses *bah*·hos
New Zealand	**Nueva Zelanda** *nweh*·bah theh·*lahn*·dah
Northern Ireland	**Irlanda del Norte** eer·*lahn*·dah del *nor*·teh
Pakistan	**Pakistán** pahkee·*stahn*
Portugal	**Portugal** portoo·*gahl*
Scotland	**Escocia** eh·*sco*·thyah

South Africa	**Sudáfrica** soo·*dah*·freecah
Spain	**España** eh·*spah*·nyah
Switzerland	**Suiza** *swee*·thah
United States	**Estados Unidos** eh·*stah*·dos oo·*nee*·dos
Wales	**Gales** *gah*·les
West Indies	**Antillas** ahn·*tee*·yahs

Nationalities

Where two alternatives are given, the first is used for males, the second for females.

American	**americano/americana** ahmehri·*cah*·no/ahmehri·*cah*·nah
Australian	**australiano/australiana** ah·oostrah·*lyah*·no/ ah·oostrah·*lyah*·nah
British	**británico/británica** bri·*tah*·nico/bri·*tah*·nicah
Canadian	**canadiense** cahnah·*dyen*·seh
East African	**africano/africana del este** ahfree·*cah*·no/ahfree·*cah*·nah del *eh*·steh
English	**inglés/inglesa** in·*glehs*/in·*gleh*·sah
French	**francés/francesa** frahn·*thehs*/frahn·*theh*·sah
German	**alemán/alemana** ahleh·*mahn*/ahleh·*mah*·nah
Indian	**hindú** in·*doo*
Irish	**irlandés/irlandesa** eerlahn·*dehs*/eerlahn·*deh*·sah
New Zealander	**neozelandés/neozelandesa** neh·o·theh·lahn·*dehs*/ neh·o·theh·lahn·*deh*·sah
Pakistani	**pakistaní** pahkee·stah·*nee*

Scots	**escocés/escocesa** ehsco·*thehs*/ehsco·*theh*·sah
South African	**sudafricano/sudafricana** soodahfree·*cah*·no/ soodahfree·*cah*·nah
Welsh	**galés/galesa** gah·*lehs*/gah·*leh*·sah
West Indian	**antillano/antillana** ahntee·*yah*·no/ahntee·*yah*·nah

Department Store Guide

Alfombras	Carpets, rugs
Alimentación	Food
Artículos de deporte	Sports
Artículos de limpieza	Cleaning materials
Artículos de montaña	Mountaineering department
Artículos de piel	Leather goods
Artículos de playa	Beach accessories
Artículos de viaje	Travel articles
Baterías de cocina	Kitchen utensils
Blusas	Blouses
Bolsos	Handbags, purses
Bricolaje	Do-it-yourself
Caballeros	Menswear
Cafetería	Café
Caja	Cash register, checkout
Caliente (C)	Hot [*water*]
Camisas	Shirts
Camisería	Shirt department
Camping	Camping
CDs	Compact discs
Cinturones	Belts
Cojines	Cushions
Corbatas	Ties
Cortinas	Curtains
Cosméticos	Cosmetics
Cristalería	Glassware
Cuarto/Cuarta	Fourth
Cubiertas	Coverlets
Discos	Records
Droguería	Toiletries
Electrodomésticos	Household appliances

Fajas	Girdles
Ferretería	Hardware
Fotografía	Photography
Frío (F)	Cold [*water*]
Guantes	Gloves
Hogar	Home furnishings
Información	Information
Jardinería	Gardening
Jerseys	Sweaters
Joyería	Jewelry
Juguetes	Toys
Laminados	Laminates
Lencería	Lingerie
Librería	Books
Loza	Earthenware
Mantas	Blankets
Mantelerías	Table linens
Medias	Stockings
Mercería	Notions
Moda juvenil	Young fashions
Modas señora	Ladies' fashions
Muebles	Furniture
Muebles de cocina	Kitchen furniture
Niños/Niñas	Children
Oportunidades	Special offers
Pañería	Drapery
Papelería	Stationery
Perfumería	Perfumery
Piso	Floor
Planta	Floor
Planta baja	Ground floor
Porcelana	China
Primero	First
Radio	Radio
Reclamaciones	Complaints
Regalos	Gifts
Relojería	Watches
Retales	Remnants
Ropa confeccionada	Ready-made clothing
Ropa de cama	Bedding
Ropa infantil	Children's wear
Ropa interior	Underwear

Sección	Department
Segundo	Second
Señora/Señoras	Ladies' fashions
Sombrerería	Millinery, hat shop
Sostenes	Bras
Sótano	Basement
Sujetadores	Bras
Tapicerías	Upholstery
Televisión	Television
Tercero	Third
Vajilla	Crockery
Ventas a crédito	Accounts
Zapatería	Footwear
Zapatillas	Slippers

Conversion Tables

Metric/U.S. systems

To convert from the metric to the U.S. system, read from the single digit in the center column to the number on the left; for example, 5 liters = 10.55 pints. To convert from the U.S. system to the metric, read from the single digit in the center column to the number on the right; for example, 5 pints = 2.35 liters.

PINTS		LITERS	GALLONS		LITERS
2.11	1	0.47	0.26	1	3.78
4.22	2	0.94	0.52	2	7.57
6.33	3	1.41	0.78	3	11.34
8.44	4	1.88	1.04	4	15.12
10.55	5	2.35	1.30	5	17.40
12.66	6	2.82	1.56	6	22.68
14.77	7	3.29	1.82	7	26.46
16.88	8	3.76	2.08	8	30.24
18.99	9	4.23	2.34	9	34.02

OUNCES		GRAMS	POUNDS		KILOS
0.04	1	28.35	2.20	1	0.45
0.07	2	56.70	4.41	2	0.91
0.11	3	85.05	6.61	3	1.36
0.14	4	113.40	8.82	4	1.81
0.18	5	141.75	11.02	5	2.27
0.21	6	170.10	13.23	6	2.72
0.25	7	198.45	15.43	7	3.18
0.28	8	226.80	17.64	8	3.63
0.32	9	255.15	19.84	9	4.08

INCHES		CENTIMETERS	YARDS		METERS
0.39	1	2.54	1.09	1	0.91
0.79	2	5.08	2.19	2	1.83
1.18	3	7.62	3.28	3	2.74
1.58	4	10.16	4.37	4	3.66
1.95	5	12.70	5.47	5	4.57
2.36	6	15.24	6.56	6	5.49
2.76	7	17.78	7.66	7	6.40
3.15	8	20.32	8.65	8	7.32
3.54	9	22.86	9.84	9	8.23

MILES		KILOMETERS
0.62	1	1.61
1.24	2	3.22
1.86	3	4.83
2.49	4	6.44
3.11	5	8.05
3.73	6	9.66
4.35	7	11.27
4.97	8	12.87
5.59	9	14.48

To convert kilometers to miles, divide by 8 and multiply by 5. To convert miles to kilometers, divide by 5 and multiply by 8.

Temperature

FAHRENHEIT (°F)	CELSIUS (°C)	
212°	100°	boiling point of water
100°	38°	
98.6°	37°	body temperature
86°	30°	
77°	25°	
68°	20°	
59°	15°	
50°	10°	
41°	5°	
32°	0°	freezing point of water
14°	−10°	
−4°	−20°	

To convert degrees Celsius to degrees Fahrenheit, divide by 5, multiply by 9, and add 32. To convert degrees Fahrenheit to degrees Celsius: subtract 32, divide by 9, and multiply by 5.

Tire Pressure

POUNDS PER SQUARE INCH	KILOGRAMS PER SQUARE CENTIMETER
18	1.3
20	1.4
22	1.5
25	1.7
29	2.0
32	2.3
35	2.5
36	2.5
39	2.7
40	2.8
43	3.0
45	3.2
46	3.2
50	3.5
60	4.2

Clothing Sizes

Always try clothes on before buying. Clothing sizes in conversion tables are often unreliable.

Women's Dresses and Suits

Continental Europe	38	40	42	44	46	48
U.K.	32	34	36	38	40	42
U.S.	10	12	14	16	18	20

Men's Suits, Coats, and Jackets

Continental Europe	46	48	50	52	54	56
U.K./U.S.	36	38	40	42	44	46

Men's Shirts

Continental Europe	36	37	38	39	41	42	43
U.K./U.S.	14	14½	15	15½	16	16½	17

Socks

Continental Europe	38–39	39–40	40–41	41–42	42–43
U.K./U.S.	9½	10	10½	11	11½

Shoes

Continental Europe	34	35½	36½	38	39
U.K.	2	3	4	5	6
U.S.	3½	4½	5½	6½	7½
Continental Europe	41	42	43	44	45
U.K.	7	8	9	10	11
U.S.	8½	9½	10½	11½	12½

Do It Yourself: Some Notes on the Spanish Language

This section does not deal with "grammar" as such. The purpose here is to explain some of the most useful and elementary nuts and bolts of the language, based on the principal phrases included in the book. This information should enable you to produce numerous sentences of your own making.

There is no pronunciation guide in most of this section, partly because it would get in the way of the explanations and partly because you have to do it yourself at this stage if you are serious. You can use the earlier examples in this book to figure out the pronunciation of the Spanish words in this section.

"The"

All nouns in Spanish belong to one of two genders—masculine or feminine—regardless of whether they refer to living beings or inanimate objects.

"the" (SINGULAR)	MASCULINE	FEMININE
the address		**la dirección**
the apple		**la manzana**
the check/bill		**la cuenta**
the cup of tea		**la taza de té**
the glass of wine	**el vaso de vino**	
the key		**la llave**
the luggage	**el equipaje**	
the menu	**el menú**	
the newspaper	**el periódico**	
the receipt	**el recibo**	
the sandwich	**el bocadillo**	
the suitcase		**la maleta**
the telephone directory		**la guía telefónica**
the schedule	**el horario**	

- "The" is **el** before most masculine nouns and **la** before most feminine nouns.

- You can often tell if a singular noun is masculine or feminine by its ending. Masculine nouns usually end in *o* and feminine nouns in *a*. But there are many exceptions, notably a whole group of nouns that end in *e*, for example, **el equipaje**, so you should learn the gender of nouns as you learn the nouns themselves. If you read a word with **el** or **la** in front of it, you can detect its gender immediately: **el menú** is masculine (*m.* or *masc.* in dictionaries) and **la dirección** is feminine (*f.* or *fem.* in dictionaries).

- Does it matter? Not unless you want to make a serious attempt to speak correctly and scratch beneath the surface of the language. You would be understood if you said **la menú** or even **el dirección**, provided your pronunciation was good.

"the" (PLURAL)	MASCULINE	FEMININE
the addresses		**las direcciones**
the apples		**las manzanas**
the checks/bills		**las cuentas**
the cups of tea		**las tazas de té**
the glasses of wine	**los vasos de vino**	
the keys		**las llaves**
the luggage	(*no plural*)	
the menus	**los menús**	
the newspapers	**los periódicos**	
the receipts	**los recibos**	
the sandwiches	**los bocadillos**	
the suitcases		**las maletas**
the telephone directories		**las guías telefónicas**
the schedules	**los horarios**	

- Most nouns add an *s* when they are made plural. However, a noun ending in a consonant adds *es*, for example, **la dirección, las direcciones.**

- "The" is **los** before masculine nouns in the plural.

- "The" is **las** before feminine nouns in the plural.

Practice saying and writing the following sentences in Spanish.

Do you have the key?	**¿Tiene usted la llave?**
Do you have the luggage?	**¿Tiene usted…?**
Do you have the telephone directory?	
Do you have the menu?	

I would like the key.	**Quiero la llave.**
I would like the receipt.	**Quiero....**
I would like the check/bill.	
I would like the keys.	
Where is the key?	**¿Dónde está la llave?**
Where is the schedule?	**¿Dónde está...?**
Where is the address?	
Where is the suitcase?	
Where is the luggage?	
Where are the keys?	**¿Dónde están las llaves?**
Where are the sandwiches?	**¿Dónde están...?**
Where are the apples?	
Where are the suitcases?	
Where can I get the key?	**¿Dónde puedo obtener la llave?**
Where can I get the address?	**¿Dónde puedo obtener...?**
Where can I get the schedules?	

Now try to make up more sentences along the same lines. Try adding "please" (**por favor**) at the end.

"A"/"An" and "Some"/"Any"

"a"/"an" (SINGULAR)	MASCULINE	FEMININE
an address		**una dirección**
an apple		**una manzana**
a check/bill		**una cuenta**
a cup of tea		**una taza de té**
a glass of wine	**un vaso de vino**	
a key		**una llave**
a menu	**un menú**	
a newspaper	**un periódico**	
a sandwich	**un bocadillo**	
a suitcase		**una maleta**
a telephone directory		**una guía telefónica**
a schedule	**un horario**	

"some"/"any" (PLURAL)	MASCULINE	FEMININE
addresses		**unas direcciones**
apples		**unas manzanas**
checks/bills		**unas cuentas**
cups of tea		**unas tazas de té**
glasses of wine	**unos vasos de vino**	
keys		**unas llaves**
menus	**unos menús**	
newspapers	**unos periódicos**	
receipts	**unos recibos**	
sandwiches	**unos bocadillos**	
suitcases		**unas maletas**
telephone directories		**unas guías telefónicas**
schedules	**unos horarios**	

- "A" or "an" is **un** before masculine nouns and **una** before feminine nouns.

- The plural "some" or "any" is **unos** before masculine nouns and **unas** before feminine nouns.

- In certain Spanish expressions, **unos** and **unas** are omitted. Examples of this are marked by an asterisk (*) before some of the sentences below.

Practice saying and writing the following sentences in Spanish.

Do you have the receipt?	¿Tiene usted…?
Do you have a menu?	
I would like a telephone directory.	Quiero….
I would like some sandwiches.	
Where can I get some newspapers?	¿Dónde puedo obtener…?
Where can I get a cup of tea?	
Is there a key?	¿Hay una llave?
Is there a schedule?	¿Hay…?
Is there a telephone directory?	
Is there a menu?	
Are there any keys?	¿Hay unas llaves?
Are there any newspapers?	¿Hay…?
Are there any sandwiches?	

Now make up your own sentences along the same lines.

Try the following new phrases.

I'll have …	**Tomo…**
I need …	**Necesito…**
I'll have a glass of wine.	**Tomo un vaso de vino.**
I'll have some sandwiches.	**Tomo….**
I'll have some apples.	
I need a cup of tea.	**Necesito una taza de té.**
I need a key.	**Necesito….**
*I need some keys.	**Necesito llaves.**
*I need some addresses.	**Necesito….**
*I need some sandwiches.	
*I need some suitcases.	

In cases where "some" or "any" refers to more than one thing, such as *some/any ice cream* and *some/any apples*, **unos** and **unas** are used as explained above.

some/any ice cream	**unos helados**
some/any apples	**unas manzanas**

As a guide, you can usually *count* the number of containers or whole items.

In cases where "some" refers to part of a whole thing or an indefinite quantity, the words **unos** and **unas** are not used.

the beer	**la cerveza**	some beer	**cerveza**
the bread	**el pan**	some bread	**pan**
the butter	**la mantequilla**	some butter	**mantequilla**
the cheese	**el queso**	some cheese	**queso**

• The noun in these cases is always singular.

The same would apply to the following words. Can you complete the list below?

the coffee	**el café**	some coffee	_____
the sugar	**el azúcar**	some sugar	_____
the flour	**la harina**	some flour	_____
the tea	**el té**	some tea	_____
the lemonade	**la limonada**	some lemonade	_____
the water	**el agua**	some water	_____
the oil	**el aceite**	some oil	_____
the wine	**el vino**	some wine	_____

Practice saying and writing the following sentences in Spanish.

Do you have some coffee?	**¿Tiene usted café?**
Do you have some flour?	
Do you have some sugar?	
I would like some butter.	**Quiero mantequilla.**
I would like some oil.	
I would like some bread.	
Is there any lemonade?	**¿Hay limonada?**
Is there any water?	
Is there any wine?	
Where can I get some cheese?	**¿Dónde puedo obtener queso?**
Where can I get some flour?	
Where can I get some water?	
I'll have some beer.	**Tomo cerveza.**
I'll have some tea.	
I'll have some coffee.	

"This" and "That"

Spanish uses **esto** for "this" and **eso** for "that." If you do not know the Spanish word for something, just point to the object and say the following.

I would like that.	**Quiero eso.**
I'll have that.	**Tomo eso.**
I need this.	**Necesito esto.**

Helping Others

You can help yourself by using sentences such as the following.

I would like a sandwich.	**Quiero un bocadillo.**
Where can I get a cup of tea?	**¿Dónde puedo obtener una taza de té?**
I'll have a glass of wine.	**Tomo un vaso de vino.**
I need a receipt.	**Necesito un recibo.**

If you encounter a speaker of English who is having trouble making himself or herself understood, you should be able to speak Spanish on the person's behalf.

It is not necessary to say the words for "he" (**él**), "she" (**ella**), and "I" (**yo**) in Spanish unless you want to emphasize them (as in "*He'll* have a beer, and *I'll* have a glass of wine").

He would like ….	**(Él) quiere un bocadillo.** (el) kee·*eh*·reh oon bocah·*dee*·yo
She would like ….	**(Ella) quiere un bocadillo.** (*eh*·yah) kee·*eh*·reh oon bo·cah·*dee*·yo
Where can he get …?	**¿Dónde puede (él) obtener una taza de té?** *don*·deh *pweh*·deh (el) obteh·*nehr* oo·nah *tah*·thah deh teh
Where can she get …?	**¿Dónde puede (ella) obtener una taza de té?** *don*·deh *pweh*·deh (*eh*·yah) obteh·*nehr* oo·nah *tah*·thah deh teh
He'll have ….	**(Él) toma un vaso de vino.** (el) *to*·mah oon *bah*·so deh *bee*·no
She'll have ….	**(Ella) toma un vaso de vino.** (*eh*·yah) *to*·mah oon *bah*·so deh *bee*·no
He needs ….	**(Él) necesita un recibo.** (el) neh·theh·*see*·tah oon reh·*thee*·bo
She needs ….	**(Ella) necesita un recibo.** (*eh*·yah) neh·theh·*see*·tah oon reh·*thee*·bo

You can also help two or more people if they are having difficulties. The Spanish words for "they" are **ellos** (male) and **ellas** (female), with **ellos** also used for a group that includes both males and females. These words are usually omitted. Instead, the verb ending changes for "they."

They'd like ….	**(Ellos) quieren queso.** (*eh*·yos) kee·*eh*·ren *keh*·so
They'd like ….	**(Ellas) quieren queso.** (*eh*·yahs) kee·*eh*·ren *keh*·so
Where can they get …?	**¿Dónde pueden obtener mantequilla?** *don*·deh *pweh*·den obteh·*nehr* mahnteh·*kee*·yah
They'll have ….	**Toman vino.** *to*·mahn *bee*·no
They need ….	**Necesitan agua.** neh·theh·*see*·tahn *ah*·gwah

What about the two of you? No problem. The words for "we" are **nosotros** (male) and **nosotras** (female), but they are usually omitted. Instead, the verb ending changes for "we."

We would like ….	**Queremos vino.** keh·*reh*·mos *bee*·no
Where can we get …?	**¿Dónde podemos obtener agua?** *don*·deh po·*deh*·mos obteh·*nehr* *ah*·gwah
We'll have ….	**Tomamos cerveza.** to·*mah*·mos thehr·*beh*·thah
We need ….	**Necesitamos azúcar.** neh·theh·see·*tah*·mos ah·*thoo*·car

Try writing out your own checklist for these four useful sentence-starters, like the following.

Quiero….	**Queremos….**
Quiere (él)….	**Quieren (ellos)….**
Quiere (ella)….	**Quieren (ellas)….**
¿Dónde puedo obtener…?	**¿Dónde… obtener…?**
¿Dónde puede (él) obtener…?	**¿Dónde… (ellos) obtener…?**
¿Dónde puede (ella) obtener…?	**¿Dónde… (ellas) obtener…?**

More Practice

Here are some more Spanish names of things. Using the information given above, see how many different sentences you can make up.

	SINGULAR	PLURAL
ashtray	**cenicero** (*masc.*)	**ceniceros**
bag	**bolsa** (*fem.*)	**bolsas**
car	**coche** (*masc.*)	**coches**
cigarette	**cigarrillo** (*masc.*)	**cigarrillos**
corkscrew	**sacacorchos** (*masc.*)	**sacacorchos**
garage (*repairs*)	**garaje** (*masc.*)	**garajes**
grape	**uva** (*fem.*)	**uvas**
ice cream	**helado** (*masc.*)	**helados**
knife	**cuchillo** (*masc.*)	**cuchillos**
melon	**melón** (*masc.*)	**melones**
passport	**pasaporte** (*masc.*)	**pasaportes**
postcard	**tarjeta postal** (*fem.*)	**tarjetas postales**
salad	**ensalada** (*fem.*)	**ensaladas**
shoe	**zapato** (*masc.*)	**zapatos**

stamp	**sello** (*masc.*)	**sellos**
station	**estación** (*fem.*)	**estaciones**
street	**calle** (*fem.*)	**calles**
sunglasses	(*no singular*)	**gafas de sol** (*fem.*)
telephone	**teléfono** (*masc.*)	**teléfonos**
ticket	**billete** (*masc.*)	**billetes**

Index

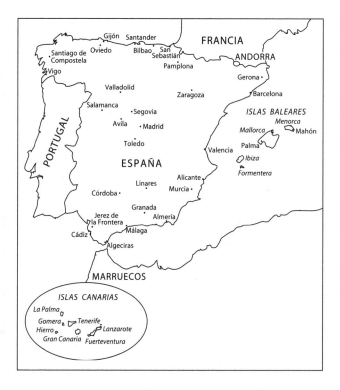